Escaping Ice-Prison

From City to Steppe in Mongolia

PAUL BACON

This book was originally written and published in 2005. However, this new edition is dedicated to my amazing wife, Tracy. I hope to take you to the Land of the Blue Skies one day soon.

CONTENTS

PROLOGUE

The story of my adventures in Mongolia doesn't actually begin on the sweeping grasslands of northern Asia but, rather, in the broad acres of Yorkshire and actually commences well over a year before I even arrived in Ulaan Baatar. After having graduated university, I was living at home and working in a magnificently boring entry-level marketing job in order to save money to travel. Although, in all honesty, the word 'travel' was still a rather undefined and vague concept. At the point where we begin, I still had no great idea as to where I wanted to go or what I intended to do whilst I was there. I had considered returning to the US, where I had spent the third year of my university course, and had also mulled over the idea of teaching in Africa. But, I was nowhere really close to booking a flight anywhere.. I only decided that Mongolia would be my ultimate destination thanks to a rather random moment that took place in Sheffield city centre.

It was lunchtime on a warm and sunny spring afternoon and I was walking through Sheffield to get my lunch. As I ambled along the city's main pedestrian thoroughfare enjoying the sunshine, a Big Issue seller pounced upon me. I am a little ashamed to admit that I wasn't so keen to part with £1.50 and so I tried to fob the young man off by telling him that I had no change. He responded, quick as a flash, by telling me that he had change for both a £5 note and a £10 note. It was the perfect retort and I felt that I would be a genuinely terrible person if I refused to buy a copy. Even though I didn't have the greatest job in the world, my situation was certainly better than his. So, I ponied up my cash!

As I didn't find the Big Issue particularly interesting reading, I slipped it into my work bag and forgot about it. It was not until a month or so later, when I cleaned the bag out, that I came across the magazine. The majority of what I read was not at all interesting. However, when I reached the back cover, my interest was piqued by an advertisement for an adventure travel company that organised volunteer projects overseas. It seemed to be just the type of thing I was looking for. So, I took a look at their website and did a little research.

The company, I to I, had a fantastic array of different projects in lots of different exotic countries around the world. It all looked cool and I was drawn in almost immediately. There were lots of projects in Africa and Southeast Asia doing charity style work: building schools, digging wells and that type of thing. However, when I saw that they also had projects in Mongolia, I knew I had found what I was looking for. There were opportunities to teach English or to do youth work projects, but my eyes were drawn to a project working in Mongolian media!

My time in Mongolia would prove to be fabulous. The vast yet almost anonymous country between Russia and China was - in almost equal parts - beautiful, fascinating, frustrating and heartbreaking. I had amazing adventures in some of the most magnificent natural settings you can imagine. I also met some really interesting people and got involved in some weird and wonderful activities. Simultaneously, I saw some horrific corruption and some genuinely awful social problems. Despite some of those ups and downs, the time I spent in the 'Land of the Blue Skies' was some of the greatest of my life. I don't wish to sound like a tourist brochure, but I did and saw things that were totally unique and created memories that will stay with me forever. I sincerely hope the following pages will do my experiences justice and will give you a window into one of the world's last genuinely unexplored countries.

1. AT HOME WITH THE BATMUNKHS

As wonderful as my time in Mongolia was, it began under a huge cloud of ignorance. I had booked the trip pretty much straight after I saw the advertisement in the Big Issue because it looked like it would be an amazing adventure. The problem was, though, that it was difficult to get too much tangible and practical information about life in Mongolia. I already knew where the country was and that it got really cold in the winter, but Google didn't really give me too much more. There were lots of beautiful pictures of rolling grasslands, of horsemen flying across the steppe and of wrestlers wearing bizarre outfits. There was also plenty of information about Chinggis Khan (The Mongolian spelling) and his global conquests. Unfortunately, there wasn't too much information about contemporary Ulan Baatar.

Thankfully, I-to-I were able to provide me with some information about the practicalities of my trip. For example, I knew that I would be working for an English language newspaper and would be living with a Mongolian family called the Batmunkhs in their apartment on Sansar Boulevard in the Bayanzurkh district of the city, but I had no idea exactly where Bayanzurkh was and whether it would be a nice place to live. I also knew that the Batmunkhs were a family of four: There was Mr. Batmunkh who worked as a civil servant in the Mongolia parliament, there was his wife Oyuntsetseg (Or Oyuna for short) who was a housewife, his son Bimba who studied at university, and his daughter Handmaa who went to Kindergarten.

I also managed to get a clear picture of some of the picture of some of the dangers involved in travelling to a country as wild and under-developed as Mongolia. The first aspect of this came when I visited my local GP to check if I needed any vaccinations ahead of the trip.

"Where is it you are going? Mongolia you say? That sounds rather exciting. Let me see what you will need. Hmmmm. It seems you will have to have everything basically".

"Everything?"

"Yes. Typhoid, hepatitis and all those. The vaccination guide also recommends rabies too".

"Ok, wow!"

"Actually, in all practicality, you probably don't need Japanese Encephalitis. But, I would definitely get all the rest".

In the months preceding the trip, I spent way more time than I would ordinarily have liked at the GP getting all manner of injections - the rabies vaccination alone was three separate shots.

The second aspect was the need for some pretty sturdy and

comprehensive travel insurance. Lonely Planet said, quite bluntly, "If ever there was a country where you needed travel insurance, Mongolia is it". It warned about the dangerous combination of wild countryside, minimal infrastructure and poorly organized travel agencies. It also recommended having extra medical provisions that would allow you to be air-lifted out of the country to Russia or China in the event of illness or a serious accident. Apparently, it was not wise to seek treatment in a Mongolian hospital.

This information was all very safety focused. It was all good to know, but I hoped it would not be something that I actually needed whilst I was in Mongolia. As useful as it was, I also wanted to know things that I could use on a more practical level. I wanted to know what it would be like to live in Ulaan Baatar on a day to day level. Was there a lot to do? Was it a good place to go for a night out? Were there any good restaurants? If so, what kind of food might I find? Would there be any opportunities to play some sport? These were the questions I found really difficult to answer.

As I am always a big fan of being prepared for any type of travel, I was pretty frustrated at not knowing all I could about my trip. I-to-I emphasized that this was perfectly normal for Mongolia as it was not a country blessed with great communications infrastructure or practices, and that I should think about getting used to operating in the dark. They explained that it was totally run of the mill for letters to be left undelivered - my own visa application had issues in that regard - for the internet to often crash and for phone calls to be randomly cut off.

Travelling to Mongolia

Mongolia is a pretty remote country. It is the size of France and Germany combined and sits wedged between Russia's far western region - where Stalin and the Tsars before him exiled undesirable elements - and some of China's less populated western provinces. Because of this, it is not the easiest place to reach. It took me the best part of 36 hours to get there. This took in a flight from London to Moscow, a 20-hour layover at Sheremetyevo airport and then an eight-hour flight from Moscow to Ulaan Baatar. I flew into Mongolia on a rather dated Aeroflot aircraft. It was not like flying on Emirates or Cathay Pacific! For the eight-hour flight to Ulaan Baatar, the only form of in-flight entertainment was the complementary vodka that was handed out at dramatically regular intervals. There was no TV, no movies, just vodka. As I passed over Siberia, I peered out of the window beside me – there was precious little else to do - and looked down on a vast expanse of snow, ice and frozen wilderness. I could see nothing for miles around. It looked cold, very cold.

The expanse of frozen nothingness stretched for miles and miles. It wasn't until over seven hours into the flight that any signs of civilization appeared. Just off to the right of the plane, I noticed an unsightly dark spot in the otherwise cloudless blue sky and the pristine white earth. As the plane banked round, the smudge began to grow in size and I soon realized that the blot on the landscape before me was Ulaan Baatar. As we drew closer, I began to see that above the city hung a dense cloud of thick, dirty smog. It wasn't the best of first impressions!

From the air, UB certainly hadn't appeared to be the most inviting of cities. This impression continued to grow once we were on the ground ... in many ways! As we touched down, the flight attendant calmly announced that we had landed safely, the local time was just before nine and that outside it was minus 22 degrees. Even the mention of a temperature that cold sent a vicious chill through my entire body and had me wondering whether the winter clothing I had bought in the UK was going to cut the mustard.

After making it to the arrivals hall, I was greeted by Sogi (a representative from I-to-I's partner, The Mongolian Youth Development Fund) who quickly whisked me into a cab, out of the biting cold and off towards the city. The drive from the airport took around twenty minutes and gave me a brief glimpse of Ulaan Baatar and the surrounding areas. It seemed pretty grim. Actually, no, it seemed very grim. The road into the city was paved, but took up only a single carriageway and was very bumpy. It ran parallel to several aging and rather decrepit looking industrial facilities that appeared to be making their best efforts at maintaining the cloud of smog through which I had flown an hour or so earlier.

After about twenty minutes driving through the rather depressing outskirts of the city, we drew towards Sukhbaatar Square, the focal point of Ulaan Baatar and the home of the Mongolian

Parliament, or Great Khural. From my copy of Lonely Planet, I had learned that it was named after Damdin Sukhbaatar, Mongolia's revolutionary hero who was instrumental in the country's struggle for independence from China in the 1920s. In 1990, it was also home to the pro-democracy demonstrations that followed on from the revolutions in Eastern Europe and brought the demise of the totalitarian Soviet-backed Communist regime.

Thankfully, the square brought a little more colour into the journey. It was surrounded on three sides by rather imposing looking buildings that could easily have been used in an architecture class as examples of the blunt lines and overblown scale of Communist architecture. However, despite their rather dramatic and imposing stature, the majority of them were painted in some rather delicate pastel shades, which seemed to make everything a little more cheerful. The central Post Office was a tasteful, but slightly faded canary yellow. The National Opera House was a light orange. And, the Children's Palace across the street was a striking reddish ochre.

After the square, we turned onto Peace Avenue, which is Ulaan Baatar's main traffic artery. Sogi was keen to tell me that it was the busiest road for over 1,500km in any direction. She did this with a look of immense pride on her face. In my exhausted and jet-lagged state, this seemed like quite an impressive statistic and I nodded approvingly. However, as in pretty much every direction Ulaan Baatar is surrounded by vast expanses of steppe and desert, there is not actually that much competition. On that cold Saturday morning, though, Peace Avenue was relatively empty, which allowed me to get a good glimpse of my new surroundings.

The first building we passed was another slab-fronted lump: the Ulaan Baatar Hotel, Mongolia's biggest hotel. The brutish lines and featureless facade really didn't make it look too appealing to weary travellers. In fact, the lack of a pastel makeover made it feel genuinely depressing. However, I only looked at the hotel for a matter of seconds before my eyes were drawn away by something standing defiantly in front of it: a giant statue of Lenin. It looked to be over 30m in height and dominated the view. I was left dumbstruck. I knew Mongolia had a complex history in regards to Communism - this is a theme that will appear a lot in the pages of this book as even more than a decade after the collapse of the system, it still left a huge imprint on the country - but I was surprised to find Voldoya himself staring out at me on my first morning in the city.

It seemed very strange that such a relic would still be in such a prominent position. It was, let's not forget stationed on the busiest road for 1,500km, in front of the country's largest hotel! Mongolia was under Communist rule from 1924 until 1992, Just as with the former Soviet Union and some of the Eastern European satellite states, it was a horrific tale that featured murderous purges as well as political repression and economic stagnation. Yet, there was the architect of it all surveying a country that his ideology had left in tatters. I did not know it at the time, but his continued presence on Peace Avenue said a lot about the direction in which the country was and had been travelling.

After Lenin slid out of view and we had travelled a further three or four kilometres along Peace Avenue away from the centre of the city, we took a left turning and headed up Sansar Boulevard. Much to my dismay, the motif of brutish Communist-era architecture continued to assert itself. Sadly, the suburban version did not quite match the grandeur of Sukhbaatar Square. Sansar was lined with a series of apartment blocks that looked like a collection of rather shabby lime-green lego bricks. In the bright morning light, they were looking a little worse for wear. The paint was badly faded and the brickwork looked as though it were crumbling away in several places. There were five of these buildings, none of which looked at all inviting. As our taxi laboured up the avenue, Sogi looked across at the blocks and told me that the fourth one along was to be my home for the next few months. My heart sank and I began to feel a little nervous.

As I dragged my over-sized backpack out of the taxi and into the greying snow at the side of the road, I was struck first by the biting cold and then by the grim appearance of my new home. It really did not look good! There was a large rusting door to the block that was insulated with a heavy felt covering that made it immensely difficult to open. The lobby was dimly lit by two uncovered light bulbs that dangled from a hole in the roof. The walls were covered in dirty chipped paint and the floor was awash in melting snow and filth. There were two lifts that served the twelve floors of apartments, neither of which looked at all safe. One had a cracked button to call it, the other just an exposed wire. I looked at them apprehensively as we crossed the floor, but thankfully Sogi motioned for me to carry on past them and head for the stairs.

The stairwell was not lit. Instead, it relied on the residual light provided by the already overworked bulbs in the lobby. As I dragged my bag over the dirty steps, I could make out piles of plastic bags full of garbage, scores of empty vodka bottles and a few piles of unidentified animal bones on the floor. We got to the first floor and shuffled into a darkened corridor. Whilst Sogi searched for the door to the Batmunkhs' apartment, I heard the elevator rumble past making some mildly alarming noises. As she found the door and thumped on the bare wood with her gloved hand – the bell was not working - I was feeling a little apprehensive about my surroundings. However, I didn't have too long to dwell on my fears as Sogi's knock was greeted by a great deal of shouting and banging from inside. Eventually, this commotion died down and a short, thickset Mongolian lady of about forty opened the door. She was wearing a pair of pink, but distinctly grimy looking pyjamas. This was Oyuntsetseg, or Oyuna as I was instructed to call her. I was 'home'.

Arriving at 'home'

Even before entering the apartment block, I had been pretty worried about where I would be living. The filthy lobby and stairs, that were for some reason covered in animal bones, had done little to assuage this. So, as Oyuna ushered me through the door and I took off my heavy winter boots, my eyes were flitting around nervously to take in my new surroundings.

I soon found that Chez Batmunkh had two main rooms: a living room and a bedroom. I was to sleep in the bedroom whilst the remainder of the family would use the living room. Thankfully, my room was pleasant enough and negated many of the fears that the lobby and staircase had created in my mind – no rats or dismembered animals. Even though it was decorated in some ageing and in places peeling wallpaper, it was clean and perfectly habitable. I had a fold out bed, a small desk, and a sizable TV (I later found that it showed nothing except Mongolian, Russian or Chinese TV).

After I dumped my bags in the room and showered two flights and one lengthy layover off my skin, I went to sit with the family in the main room. We exchanged handshakes and polite smiles, but, alas, little else in terms of communication. After a few minutes of early euphoria, came one of the lengthiest uncomfortable silences I have ever endured. Batmunkh and Oyuna had greeted me warmly and were offering me a constant stream of food and tea, but they spoke no English. Literally, not a word beyond "Hello". So, for about three hours, I sat on the edge of the couch smiling nervously as they stared intently at me. I was left desperately awaiting the evening when Bimba would return from his day's studies at the technical college. According to Sogi he spoke a little English and hopefully we would be able to hold at least a basic conversation.

When the evening did come around, I finally met Bimba. Unfortunately, I soon discovered that when Sogi said "a little English" she actually meant "very little English". As I shared my first full meal with the family, we desperately tried to engineer a conversation with the use of Bimba's dictionary and my rudimentary phrasebook. We struggled and ultimately failed. It took us nearly half an hour to establish that I was in Mongolia to work for a newspaper. I did manage to locate the word *sonin* (newspaper), but was unable even to find the Mongolian for journalist – I would discover much later that it was *selguuch*. Even when I used the few Mongolian words that I could successfully identify in the book, everyone looked at me with a sense of confusion and bewilderment as my pronunciation was in need of a major overhaul. I went to bed that evening feeling content that I had a pleasant enough home in Mongolia, but also feeling very worried about how I was going to manage three months without being able to talk with my host family.

Despite the immense communication shortfall we faced, my new family was very nice and, over the subsequent three months, we got on as well as we could under the circumstances. They were tremendously hospitable. I was also surprised to find out that they were a great deal larger than I was first led to believe. In addition to the four people I had been told about, there was also a teenage girl who lived with them permanently and a girl approaching her twenties who would make fleeting appearances. The two were apparently sisters whose parents, relatives of the Batmunkhs, had been killed in a road accident. The girls had been taken in by my host family whilst Azzah (who was fifteen) finished school and her sister - whose name I never really got as I was told several different versions - attended university.

Batmunkh was the only member of the family who actually went to work. From one of our prolonged and fragmented conversations, I ascertained that he worked somewhere within the behemoth of the Mongolian Parliament, but got little in terms of specifics. Oyuna spent most of her time inside the apartment and the majority of that time wearing the same pair of pink pyjamas in which I had first seen her. However, even though she stayed home almost every day, it was actually Azzah who carried out the majority of work done in the house. She cooked most of my meals, did all of the household's washing and was generally responsible for all the cleaning that went on. It seemed as though there were some type of Dickensian arrangement in place, through which she would have a place to live in exchange for her labour in the home. I cannot say I ever felt 100% comfortable with her doing all my laundry and cleaning my room everyday. But, as I could not even exchange basic pleasantries with them, I certainly could not communicate my misgivings and certainly didn't understand the ins and outs of the situation.

Getting a taste for Mongolian cuisine

For the duration of my stay in Mongolia, my family made me two meals a day. They - or more specifically Azzah - cooked me almost every type of Mongolian food in the process. Unfortunately, the native cuisine was less than varied and the majority of my meals were based around one central ingredient: mutton. Almost everything the average Mongolian eats contains it. I really cannot emphasize this point enough. It may seem like an exaggeration but, on some days, all three meals were mutton-based. This probably sounds like I am doing Mongolian cuisine a massive disservice as I have painted it as stodgy and frighteningly one-dimensional, but my time with the Batmunkhs highlighted that there really wasn't too much variety to the local grub and that it was unbelievably heavy!

Azzah's speciality was Tsuiven, a combination of mutton, carrots, potatoes and noodles that, although quite bland, was usually enjoyable. I also regularly sampled the national dish, a type of mutton dumpling known as *Buuz*, which are made with a lump of fatty minced mutton seasoned with onions wrapped in soft pastry. At this point, it is important to clarify that when I use the word 'dumpling' I am not describing something similar to the delicate morsels you can purchase at a good Chinese restaurant. The delicate pastry and varied fillings are in a totally different world to the Mongolian version in which the pastry is thick and coarse and the meat is tough and greasy. To put the Mongolian version into context, they are great for fuelling up if you plan to spend the afternoon herding sheep in freezing conditions out on the steppe, but are not so great if you are looking for a nuanced dining experience.

The first few times I ate *buuz* I was shocked by the warm burst of fat that would explode in my mouth when I bit into one. As it digested, I could almost feel my arteries clogging. My family was content to eat *buuz* at least once a day and seemed to think that it would do me good to follow suit. However, looking at Oyuna's ample frame, I grew increasingly wary of the effect a diet based around large quantities of mutton fat could have. After a week or so, my heart began to beg for a reprieve and I started looking for a way to defuse the fat explosions.

My solution was to take each dumpling and squeeze down hard on top of it so that the pastry would split and the fat would gush out into the bottom of my bowl. By the time I had finished a meal of eight or nine dumplings my bowl would be an inch deep in lukewarm fat that would otherwise have been doing my health no good whatsoever.

Life on Sansar

Whilst I was never able to communicate all that well with the Batmunkhs, I could fully appreciate the familial atmosphere that pervaded their home, even if I could only ever be something of a peripheral figure. At times, it frustrated me that I could not get closer to them and enjoy my Mongolian experience in a more complete way. This was particularly the case with Handmaa who, at only four years old, was distinctly wary of the large foreigner who had suddenly appeared in her home. On the very first day I arrived, she crept up to me slowly and offered her hand, almost averting her eyes as she did so, before scurrying back to her toys. Despite my many efforts to befriend her, even when I left the country she was still exhibiting a wonderfully shy curiosity. On countless occasions, I would sit in my room reading, watching TV, or writing in my journal when I would catch a tiny head peeking around my door. I would always stop and look back at her. When she realized that I had seen her she would disappear back to her parents emitting a tiny giggle as she went. Not even the use of strategic candy based bribes could elicit a prolonged visit. She would simply scurry into the room, take the sweet from my hand and leave as quickly as she had entered. All I ever managed from her was a hushed *sain banu* (hello) and *bayarlala* (thank you).

Despite our brief little exchanges, Handmaa fascinated me. One of my favourite parts of the day was when her mother would get her ready for kindergarten. The way they wrapped her up warm showed not only the care they took with her, but also just how cold it can get during a Mongolian winter. During the day, she wandered around the apartment in thermal leggings and a sweater, but preparing her for what was only a 50m walk became a major operation. She put a pair of trousers over her leggings before her mother forced a second sweater over the top of the one she was already wearing. This was followed by a sleeveless body warmer, a winter coat, thick boots and then an ingenious pink hat. The clever little number had two knitted flaps that, in less bone chillingly cold times, bounced on the side of her head like bunny ears, but in deep mid-winter fastened together below her chin to keep her ears and cheeks warm. The whole process took almost half an hour, whilst the walk itself took barely five minutes.

As basic as my communication with Handmaa was, it was no more limited than that I had with the rest of the household. For example, I barely spent twenty minutes with Batmunkh during my entire time in the apartment. Part of this was the fact that he was clearly the breadwinner of the family and spent a lot of time at work. However, even when he was at home, he didn't really bother trying to say too much as we couldn't communicate. To put things into context, I never learned what he actually did in parliament - he could have been a senior policy adviser or he could have cleaned the toilets - and I imagine he knew nothing about me and what I was doing in his country.

The people I spent most time with were Oyuna and Azzah. The term 'spend time' is, of course, a bit of an exaggeration as neither of them spoke English and my conversational Mongolian was reprehensible. Every day one of them would bring me my breakfast or dinner and would offer to wash my clothes, but it was very difficult to say much to either of them. The closest I got to forming any kind of relationship with either was when I brought home a box of cookies from the supermarket and we shared them whilst Azzah did the washing for the entire household and Oyuna prepared a batch of greasy dumplings.

First-world problems

Even though I liked my Mongolian home, I perpetually felt guilty for occupying one room to myself. Whilst I tucked myself up in my fold-out bed, the remaining members of the Batmunkh household all shared the living room. Batmunkh and Oyuna occupied the couch, which folded out into a bed, Bimba had a mattress by the door and Handmaa would sleep on a mat next to her mother and father. Some nights Azzah and her sister would also be squeezed into the little remaining space in the room. However, on other occasions Azzah would sit and do her homework in the kitchen, then, after she had finished, she would take her small mattress and lay down there for the night.

Obviously, I had some serious misgivings about these living conditions. For the first few days, I was desperately worried that I was taking massive advantage of the Batmunkhs. Surely, they would resent me taking so much space and leaving them in such cramped conditions! However, Sogi put the whole situation into an alarming context for me when she explained that the money the Batmunkhs received via I-to-I for playing host to me was equivalent to well over a month's salary for a Civil Servant. Therefore, they were extremely happy to give up their room for a few months. She added that she had families queueing in an extremely long line to host a foreigner as it could make a huge difference to their lives.

2. STOP THE PRESS

The difficulty in communicating with the Batmunkhs meant that, over the course of my four months in Mongolia, I did not spend all that much time at 'home'. When I did, I was limited to exchanging *sain banuus* and reading my book alone in my room. So, instead, during my free time, I tried to spend as much time as I could exploring UB and the country beyond. However, in the early stages of each week, I was taken up with my work at the UB Post.

The Post is an English-language daily newspaper that is published every week on a Thursday morning. It was run by a staff of seven people. In charge was our Editor-In-Chief Oyunbayar – or Oyun for short. She was an extremely hard-working woman who spoke great English and was keen to bring western ideas into her work. Behind Oyun were our two roving reporters, Uyanga and Bulgamaa. There was also Batmunkh who was responsible for the sports pages. The final Mongolian member of the team was

Sumya who produced a variety of articles, but made his major contribution with his page design.

The whole Mongolian side of the team was desperately keen for the Post to have a positive impact on Mongolian society and to follow western ideas of free media. However, they had very little experience with those concepts and needed significant help to polish the English in which they wrote their articles. This is where I and Shawn, the chief English editor, came in.

Up until the collapse of Communism, all of Mongolia's media was state controlled. In modern Mongolia, this is no longer the case and a free media has begun to grow. However, to describe this using the western concepts of 'freedom' and 'openness' would not be particularly appropriate. Even in the post-Communist world, the situation was rather more complex. When Communism fell and the Soviets pulled out of Mongolia, the seeds of this free media began to sprout. The problem was, though, that old ideas die hard. Even though the age of totalitarianism has passed in Mongolia, the Communist Party (The Mongolian People's Revolutionary Party) hasn't gone anywhere. They may now operate within the limits of a multi-party system, but they are still there. This meant that the playing field was not exactly as flat as it could have been. The state-controlled media still had a massive advantage over the independent organs. This dichotomy was clearly visible throughout Mongolian media, but was made extremely clear by the country's two English-language publications.

There were two English language papers: The UB Post and the Mongol Messenger. The Post was independent and was a broadsheet. The Messenger was state-run and a tabloid. Despite its shorter form, the Messenger lacked the colour and sensationalism of its western counterparts. Instead of this, it offered rather more sedate content, such as pieces dealing with developments in the country's mining industry and the international visits made by President Bagabandi. However, despite the rather stale and stagnant content, even in modern Mongolia, the Messenger easily had a far greater circulation than its independent competition.

Whereas the UB Post was popular with expats because it had the rather novel idea of putting in news stories that people might actually want to read, the Messenger had government support. Therefore, it was circulated to foreign embassies in Mongolia, Mongolian embassies overseas and all government buildings. The MPRP did not really care whether it made a profit or not – for the record, it never did – because that wasn't really the point. It was propaganda rather than news. As the government controlled the printing firms, they could print as many copies as they wanted. The battle between the two English-language papers was, in effect, Mongolian media in microcosm. It worked in the exact same way with the Mongolian-language papers. The state-run organs simply tried to bulldoze the competition using their resources and government backing rather than any journalistic devices.

With the Post facing such an uphill struggle to compete, Oyun and the other staff made every effort to give it an edge by researching and publishing stories that the government's editors would simply not allow onto their pages. This was the tactic not just of ourselves, but also of every source of independent media in Mongolia, including T.V, radio and the native-language papers. My first taste of the stark difference between state and independent media came in my very first week. On Wednesday morning, I had taken an early lunch with my fellow I-to-I volunteers Mitch (who was volunteering for the Messenger, and not loving working for the Communist Party) and Fran (who was volunteering for the state news agency Montsame and also not loving it) at which we read the freshly published issue of the Messenger. As we could have predicted, it was certainly far from controversial fare. There was a piece on agricultural subsidies and some news on Bagabandi's schedule for foreign visits in the coming year. However, that evening as we prepared the UB Post to go to press, I was lucky enough to get my teeth into some slightly different stories.

Post-Communist Corruption

The first thing I learned in the newsroom is that corruption in Mongolia is, unfortunately, extremely widespread. It is a problem that has lingered on from the previous generation of government and has permeated not just the sitting government, but opposition parties, big business — although 'big' is always a relative term in Mongolia – and almost anyone in any position of influence.

As the clock ticked towards the deadline of my first issue, Uyanga and Oyun submitted their versions of the two stories that would adorn the front-page and began my education on corruption in Mongolia. The first, which would run as the lead, dealt with the MPRP's plan to widen electoral districts. I remembered seeing this in the Messenger that morning tucked away in a corner on page 6 or somewhere similarly hidden away. I was, therefore, surprised to see Oyun decide to give it such prominence. But, I would soon see why.

The proposals were, in theory, designed to remove the possibility of 'rogue' electoral results. This was the only area on which the Messenger had focused. However, in practice, it looked remarkably like a ploy to squeeze smaller opposition parties out of contention by making the electoral districts bigger and the scope of the campaigns too large for their resources. Only one party had those kinds of resources! The opposition parties, fearful for their own futures, were not pleased with the idea and had lodged a series of stringent protests: The Motherland Coalition, The Democratic Party, the Green Party and a throng of smaller organizations had all vented their outrage at the plan. As you might expect, there had been minimal response from the government.

The second piece, which again seemed to disappear below the Messenger's radar, was a story concerning a consignment of

American aid destined for Mongolia. Earlier in the week, the US Ambassador, Pamela Slutz, had issued a statement declaring that her country would no longer deal with government offices when distributing this aid. Instead, they would work only with independent non-government organizations free of inherent corruption - although it was by no means certain that NGOs would be corruption-free either. This measure came after a string of problems with past attempts at distributing aid to Mongolia. For example, in 2003, the governor of an outlying aimag (Mongolia is split into administrative districts known as aimags similar to a province or county) had received a consignment of grain that was intended for the people under his jurisdiction. But, instead of delivering the grain, he sold it on for profit with only a tiny percentage going to the intended recipients.

My first week was nothing out of the ordinary in terms of the Post looking to print challenging and independent copy. It would be something that I was proud to be involved with for my entire time in Mongolia. I was extremely grateful that I had been placed there rather than with the Messenger. I am not sure how I would have managed working for a government propaganda organ! It was a quandary that made life slightly more difficult for my fellow volunteer Mitch, who found his project far less rewarding than I did mine. Therefore, I took every opportunity I could to learn about modern Mongolia.

After I had been in-country for a few weeks, on a rather slow news-day, I sat with Uyanga and struck up a conversation about the Post and the journalistic philosophies it adopted. We talked in great detail about challenging corruption and how we could publish the most incisive stories possible. As part of discussion, Uyanga dug out some of the paper's back issues and we discussed the impact they had had.

She believed that their crowning glory had come when the front page was adorned with faces of a dozen government figures, accompanied by suitably uncomfortable questions relating to a variety of scandals that each of the figures were involved in. The piece asked the Prime Minister, President and several cabinet ministers to account for, amongst other things, unexpected election results and missing campaign funds. As the only independent source of news in the English language, it was the type of hard journalistic currency they needed to deal in.

No country for honest men

Working for the Post helped me to get a fantastic view deep into the heart of Mongolia and deep into the heart of the problems with which it was afflicted. For example, even though corruption was widespread, blowing the whistle was no easy process. Libel was a criminal offence and an over zealous journalist could find themselves not just in trouble with their editor, but behind bars as well.

Such an incident actually took place a few weeks before I was due to arrive. A journalist from *Mongolyn Neg Odor* (A newspaper whose name roughly translates to 'One day in Mongolia') was sentenced to three months in prison for libelling the former Chairman of Ulaan Baatar's Police Department. The verdict and sentencing came, somewhat ironically, less than a week before World Press Freedom Day. As it was the Chief of Police, the quality of the hearing and the transparency of the judicial process were also somewhat questionable. However, not many journalists felt all that comfortable asking any questions about this as they may well have suffered the same fate. It highlighted what a brave move challenging the powers-that-be actually was.

Despite such events and the pervading atmosphere of intimidation, Oyun and the staff were determined to maintain an edge to the Post. The two major forces behind this were our two top reporters: Uyanga and Bulgmaa. Whilst this pairing were not quite Woodward and Bernstein, they were keen to write the type of stories that - they felt - the Mongolian people needed to hear and would not have access to in the state controlled media. Uyanga was our political correspondent. Sadly, as the previous paragraphs might suggest, she spent far more time dealing with corruption cases than she did reporting on new legislation that would actually help the Mongolian people.

The most overt of these cases was a long-running libel case between the sitting Justice Minister Ts Nyamdorj (For whom the term 'Justice' was an extremely subjective term, apparently) and the charismatic (but rather unpredictable) publicist and Democratic Party member B. Batbayar. It was a feud that painted neither individual in a particularly good light. During the course of my four month stay in Mongolia, the pair threw a series of strange allegations and threats in each other's directions. It really was a weird situation and I still wonder how much of what was said really was as bizarre as it sounded and how much was perhaps lost in translation somewhere along the way.

The first instalment of the saga that I was party to, was Nyamdorj bizarrely accusing Batbayar of labelling him as "an agent of foreign intelligence agencies". Even allowing for the fact that some of the details probably were a little bit lost in translation, this seemed somewhat off-the-wall. This was the type of thing that you would have expected in the Soviet days, but this was 2004. With such a bizarre allegation, I found polishing the English a touch difficult. So, I pushed Uyanga on the details to help me understand things a bit better and to ensure I had all the details correct - I didn't want a translation mistake to leave me and her in jail!

She explained that everything had stemmed from a sarcastic remark Batbayar had made in an interview in which he said that Nyamdorj was so incompetent at his job that it was possible that he was working for the CIA in order to undermine the Mongolian judiciary. Nyamdorj took offence to this and began the libel suit — he apparently did not see the conflict of interest or massive irony involved in the Justice Minister, a role he continued to hold throughout, being involved in the country's most high-profile libel case. Batbayar retorted that being critical of Nyamdorj's ability was truthful, but not actually libellous. This sparked a continued war of words that showed no sign of abating before I left Mongolia. The whole story was a poor reflection on Mongolian politics and everyone in the newsroom agreed that both men should have been focusing more on their day jobs than their private squabbles.

There was a second story that followed similar lines to the Nyamdorj/Batbayar affair and also featured the justice minister. However, this one not only detracted from the business of running the country, but it also took on a slightly more sinister tone. It featured the opposition MP, Lamjaviin Gundalai, a member of the Democratic Party and well-known human rights advocate who had been vociferously critical of Nyamdorj. A few weeks before I arrived in UB, he had been invited to Singapore to speak at a conference on human rights. His journey was supposed to take him to Singapore via Seoul. However, this was not to be. As the plane prepared to depart Ulaan Baatar, a detachment of government security forces burst onto the plane and dragged Gundalai and his bodyguard forcibly from their seats and off the plane. According to most reports, the security forces had no ID or arrest warrants and were seen to choke Gundalai's bodyguard.

The Democrat MP was one of the most prominent voices of opposition and had made news on a regular basis thanks to his attempts at making his views on human rights heard across Mongolia. His abduction from the aircraft proved to be a temporary, albeit damaging, set-back. He was detained just long enough to ensure he could not speak at the conference.

After his release, he was next spotted in Sukhbaatar Square outside the Great Khural on the first day of the new session of parliament. He was brandishing a banner that asked why opposition MPs would not be allowed to speak during the first day of that particular session. This was actually a pretty good question!

There were two pieces of legislation that dated back to Communist times and applied to the Khural that worked together to cause something of a quandary for the opposition M.Ps. First, the opening day of parliament was the only time at which television cameras were allowed into the Grand Khural. Second, the first day of parliament was reserved for speakers from the government. Therefore, the public would not be able to hear the opinions of the opposition MPs. The ruling MPRP were adamant that this was a mere coincidence and that it was something no-one should worry too much about. Gundalai and the other parties were not so sure.

Postscript: *With these pages being in a later edition of this book, there is an opportunity to take a brief look back at the events that followed my stay in Ulaan Baatar. Despite his dubious record, in 2005, Nyamdorj was promoted to become Chairman of the State Great Khural. However, in 2007, he was forced to resign for unilaterally changing the wording of new laws agreed in the Khural. Nyamdorj being an old-school Communist and this being the twenty-first century, one would have hoped that would have been the end of him. Sadly not. In 2017, he was appointed Justice Minister for a second time.*

Human rights issues

Alongside Uyanga and her political efforts was Bulgamaa, who took a major interest in human rights and some of the breaches that took place in Mongolia. It was Bulgamaa who had originally brought the article about US aid to the newsroom. She was also the person who introduced me to many of the major social problems that Mongolia suffered.

One area upon which Bulgamaa focused consistently was the penal system. Apparently, conditions in some of the Ulaan Baatar's prisons were horrific. Reports suggested that in many of the facilities the government did not see fit to pay for heating, which meant the prisoners faced truly freezing conditions and could easily perish over the course of the winter. In many cases, food was only supplied by the families of the prisoners. With such terrible rumours floating around, Bulgamaa was determined to see for herself. However, getting permission to visit any of the facilities proved to be next to impossible. She repeatedly made applications and was repeatedly denied for a variety of rather tenuous reasons. She tried to get into adult facilities in Ulaan Baaatar as well as some juvenile detention centres just outside the city. She must have filed 200 or 300 phone calls, none of which were ever returned.

As shocking as her work on prison conditions was, it was another article that really grabbed everyone's attention and highlighted an extremely worrying trend in modern Mongolian society, human trafficking. It examined the case of two young Mongolian women who fell foul of a vicious scheme that saw them forcibly transported to China and immersed into a situation that could justifiably be described as a living hell.

It started with the girls meeting a supposed Mongolian intermediary for a Japanese recruitment agency, who talked closely with the girls' families. These intermediaries promised jobs in Japan where the girls would be working as waitresses in nightclubs. In a country as poor as Mongolia, the opportunity presented to them was difficult to refuse. Not only would work in Japan provide glitz and glamour that they could never even hope to experience at home, but, on top of this, the salaries they were promised would make a huge difference to their families – in Japan they could probably earn three times the salary they would in Mongolia. On the surface, it seemed a no-brainer.

Sadly, all the promises proved too good to be true. They never got to Japan. Instead, they found themselves on a flight to Macau. Once they landed, they were purchased by casino owners (I do not use the term 'purchased' lightly. As Bulgamaa described it, the girls were bought and sold like slaves). After this, they were drugged by their new 'owners'. When they awoke, they found that they had been forcibly given breast implants. They were then used as unwilling prostitutes for over a year, often being forced to service scores of men in a single evening. They even faced injections that stopped them menstruating so as to leave them ready for work throughout the entirety of each month.

Their ordeal in Macau eventually came to an end when their health began to fail – a result of the sheer volume of sexual work they were forced to endure and the injections. Their owners took them to Mainland China and simply released them in the middle of the countryside. However, the nightmare did not end there. To have enough money for food and transport home, they were forced to take jobs working as prostitutes in China. However, again, their health began to fail. Fortunately, they were able to find help to travel to Beijing, where they were able to get to the Mongolian Embassy and to recount their ordeal.

Lost in translation

With stories as varied and as ground-breaking as the political and humanitarian pieces provided by Bulgamaa and Uyanga, the UB Post was generally worth the read, even if I say so myself. However, getting the appropriate information for such edgy and interesting stories was not an easy process. Therefore, to ensure that we always had something to work with, our reporters often employed the tactic of translating and borrowing information from the Mongolian language dailies (usually the independent ones).

In one respect, this worked extremely well as it allowed us to produce a wide variety of pieces and always have the best story of the week available to us. However, there was a downside to this tactic as we faced the problem of inheriting the mistakes made in other publications. If papers like Mongoliin Medee, Onodoor or

Odriin Sonin produced an article riddled with mistakes and factual inaccuracies we too would be publishing flawed copy.

Fortunately, we never inherited too many major discrepancies. However, the odd slip up was far from unknown with the chief culprit being our roving sports reporter, Batmunkh. Despite his clear enthusiasm for reporting, Batmunkh was in need of a touch of journalistic training. He produced a high volume of work for the back page, all of which was translated, but none of which was actually ever checked for mistakes.

Every week pieces were lifted from the Mongolian dailies, translated into Pidgin English and dropped into the edit tray for either Shawn or I to decipher. His crowning glory came when he wrote a piece, which took up two columns on page eight, about a highly successful Mongolian kick-boxer. It was not until two weeks later when I did a story on an athlete with the same name that it became clear that although he was a boxer, it was of the conventional kind and there was certainly no kicking involved.

Hold the back page

As Batmunkh was prone to the odd error and I am a huge sports fan, I spent a large amount of time working on stories for the back page of the paper. When I sat down for my first little editorial meeting with Batmunkh, I wasn't exactly sure what to expect in regards to sport in Mongolia. I soon discovered that I was certainly not going to be in my comfort zone as there wasn't too much in terms of traditional western sports like football, rugby or cricket. However, working with Batmunkh allowed me to learn a lot about some new sports and some very colourful sportspeople.

Mongolia surprised me with the variety of sports that made headlines. My Lonely Planet had informed me that the country traditionally favoured three 'manly' national pastimes: wrestling, archery and horse-riding. These are practised at the Naadam Festival, which takes place in July, in a fantastic extravaganza of nomadic skill. However, there were also plenty of more modern sports people making waves. These included two lightweight boxers, one of whom very briefly owned a world title, and an air-pistol shooting champion.

I found these characters quite interesting, Batmunkh and I worked on articles about Lakva Sim - one of the boxers - losing his world title to a Mexican challenger and Otryad Gundegmaa preparing for the shooting events at the Athens Olympics. However, even though these athletes were quite successful, they were almost always relegated below the fold by a character who was larger than life in almost every way possible: Dolgsurengiin Dagvadorj. Born to a family with fantastic pedigree in the world of traditional Mongolian wrestling, the young Dagvadorj was seen as talented but undisciplined when he competed as a junior in Mongolia. He was then sent to high school in Japan. Whilst he was there, he switched wrestling codes to become one of the greatest sumo wrestlers of all time.

One of the first things I had to learn whilst on the UB Post's sports beat was that sumo has a complex ranking system with five major tiers, all of which compete against each other in major tournaments known as bashos. The system is like a pyramid with lots of wrestlers in the lower sekiwake and komusubi designations and far fewer in the higher ozeki and yokozuna categories. In fact, when Batmunkh and I covered sumo, there was one yokozuna. Dagvadorj - or, Asashoryu as he was known in Japan - was by far and away sumo's top dog. We reported on Asashoryu embarking on a run that saw him win two bashos in a row without losing a single bout. By the end of the year, he had won five of the six bashos on offer. He was a genuine superstar in Mongolia as the public loved seeing him stick it to the Japanese.

The Japanese were not so keen on Asashoryu. Part of this was some good old-fashioned nationalism. They hated that their national sport was dominated so comprehensively by a foreigner. However, the second element was Asashoryu's wild side, which strongly clashed with sumo's traditional values. He had a habit of showing up late for training, brawling in bathhouses and getting into drunken arguments in his stable (Training centre). The Japanese, quite unimaginatively, labelled him 'Chinggis Khan'.

Postscript: _Batmunkh and I were fortunate to report on Asashoryu at his peak. From 2005 onwards, his star began to fade amidst allegations of alcohol abuse, match fixing and violence. His career ended in 2010 when he assaulted a waiter in a restaurant and found himself in hot water with the olice and the Japanese Sumo Association. Despite the ignominious end to his_ *competitive career, sumo treated Dagvadorj well, allowing him to amass a fortune of more than $50million. He has since invested a lot of that in companies inside Mongolia. He has also moved into politics by joining the Democratic Party.*

You would assume that Dagvadorj's decline and retirement would have been good news for the Japanese as it would allow some 'homegrown' athletes to take centre stage once more. This didn't prove to be the case as Mongolian domination continued. Whilst I was reporting on Asashoryu, I also did one or two stories about a young and gigantic pretender to the throne, Hakuho. Davarjaagal Monkhbat as he was born, started to make a few waves in 2004 before starting to win tournaments in 2006. By 2007, he too had been promoted to yokozuna. For three years between 2007 and 2010, the Mongolians held double sway over sumo. Hakuho went on to establish himself as the greatest sumo ever. He won 44 bashos, 15 of which he took without losing a match

My experiences at the post were truly enlightening. I learned so much that it almost beggars belief. It allowed me to see and understand things about Mongolian society that both shocked and amazed me. Much of the material in the following pages was accrued through my work with the Post.

3. STREETS OF ULAAN BAATAR

Mongolia is a fabulous country with fascinating culture and so many wonderful natural sights. It also has quite a spectacular and tumultuous history. It reached its peak in the thirteenth century as Chinggis Khan established one of the greatest empires the world has ever known. At its peak, it stretched from the tip of Korea to the heart of Eastern Europe. It is, therefore, no surprise that almost everything in Mongolia is named after Chinggis. There are several bars and restaurants with his name. The best brand of vodka had his image emblazoned across it, as did the country's best beer. He was also on the majority of banknotes and stamps. However, sadly for Mongolians, the days of Chinggis and his sons were very much a high-water mark. From then on, things began to ebb away dramatically.

After the empire Chinggis built collapsed under its own weight, Mongolia fell into something of a spiral. By the 1600s, it had lost its independence and fallen under Chinese rule. It would endure Chinese dominance for the best part of 300 years. There was then a brief peak in the 1920s when Sukhbaatar led Mongolia to independence, but this proved to be fleeting as the Soviet Union extended its evil tendrils in a southerly direction. Basically, no sooner had Mongolia escaped the dominance of one large and imposing neighbour, it fell under the influence of another. Like many of the other nations in close proximity to Russia, Mongolia was quickly pulled into orbit to become a Soviet satellite state, taking its political direction from Moscow and having its major decisions made within the walls of the Kremlin.

Twenty-first century Mongolia is, at long last, free from the type imperial or colonial subjugation that the Ming dynasty in China or the Soviet Union dealt in. Today, China and Russia may be influential neighbours - and you do not find too many bigger and stronger countries to share borders with - but that is all they are, neighbours. However, even though Mongolia now has its freedom and independence, it still bears some visible and highly disfiguring scars from its past. Prior to the 1990s, Mongolians had not had direct control of their own country, its systems or its economy for hundreds of years. So, when the Soviets left and took their organizational model, control and funding with them, Mongolia struggled to manage itself. Even fifteen years after the switch to democracy, the people of Ulaan Baatar and beyond were still lost in a mire of antiquated systems, institutionalised corruption and perpetuated inefficiencies.

1996 was a watershed moment. In the first few years after the collapse of the Communist system, the MPRP won the country's first democratic elections. However, in 1996 they were finally ousted by a coalition of independent parties. Hopes were high that the new guys could point the country in the right direction and begin the process of change and modernization. Unfortunately, they failed miserably in their task.

Mired in corruption, in-fighting and amateurism, the country's first genuinely democratic administration presided over a tumultuous economic collapse. This threw Mongolia into political and financial chaos. In fairness to them, this was not a unique situation. New democratic governments across the entire former Soviet sphere struggled to manage their decrepit economies in the 1990s. However, because of those troubles, in 2000 the electorate reverted to the MPRP. The party had dumped many of its more overt communist ideologies, but the people hoped it could install some of its old style control.

Inefficient infrastructure

Since the 2000 election and the reversion to the MPRP, the situation has improved. However, the country still has a long way to travel. With a weak economy and poorly maintained infrastructure, things are still in bad shape. There were days in Ulaan Baatar on which I got the impression that absolutely nothing worked and there was simply no-one around to solve any of the problems. The clearest example of this was the concrete and asphalt of the capital itself. Once the communist system began to falter, the city started to fall into a gradual state of shambolic disrepair. Roads began to crack and buildings began to crumble. No-one has, as yet, managed to halt the slide towards ruin. The prolonged neglect has left the streets riddled with potholes and the majority of apartment blocks - including the one I lived in - dingy, depressing and just a little dangerous.

The city's amenities were also in similarly ragged shape. Many Mongolians I spoke to informed me that in the mid to late 1990s power cuts were commonplace and the city spent large swathes of time drenched in darkness. In recent years, these have become less regular, but are still far from unprecedented. They were a problem I encountered regularly. At the office, when the lights went out and the computers shut down, it was a major frustration and a serious disruption to producing the paper. However, at home they rendered my apartment block treacherous and made getting in or out a precarious process.

Ordinarily, the hallway and staircase of my building was illuminated by the two small, overworked light bulbs. There was no natural light to bolster their dim glow This meant that, whatever the time of day, the ground floor was always gloomy. When the two bulbs lost their power supply though, things turned pitch black. If I arrived home in the middle of a power outage it became a major challenge to make it to my door. Feeling my way along the wall was easy enough, but it was circumnavigating the garbage - refuse collection was another area where infrastructure was poor - that lay in the stairwell and outside my neighbours' doors that proved to be a major problem. The vodka bottles and sheep bones were tricky obstacles to avoid!

Terrible transport and horrific pollution

Whilst losing power was an annoying problem, Ulaan Baatar had some deeper social and environmental issues that were in full view throughout the city. The streets of the capital are generally cold. However, as well as being wind-swept and ice-capped, they were also heavily polluted. The city was permanently covered with an overhanging cloud of smog. This ensured that the snow that settled on the ground was almost always grey rather than white. This was made clear to me even before I arrived as the cloud of smog was plain to see from the air. At ground-level, though, it looked even worse. The reasons for UB's atmospheric congestion were two-fold. Fumes were clogging the sky because of (1) the burning of vast quantities of coal for central heating, and (2) the emissions from bus and car engines.

There are approximately 40,000 vehicles on the streets of Mongolia's capital – a number which rises by almost 2,000 every year. However, the major problem was not the quantity of vehicles, but their condition. The existing transport infrastructure is one of the most visible remnants of the socialist system and many of the buses are old, unsafe and poorly maintained. Some date back to the 1980s, whilst others are imports from countries such as Korea. Sadly, they are not new and shiny Daewoos or

Hyundais. Instead, they are the vehicles that were no longer used in Korea due to their age and poor condition. The majority of these laboured along the bumpy streets, pumping clouds of diesel fumes into the already clogged atmosphere.

As poor a condition as the buses were in, they were far from the worst vehicles on the road. That dubious honour was bestowed upon the trolley buses that augmented the transit system. Ordinarily, these would not be too much of an environmental issue as they run on electricity - the majority of the electricity comes from coal-burning power stations, so the buses weren't exactly 'clean'. However, they were in such poor condition that they caused some significant issues both in terms of the transport system and the state of the city streets. They were in constant danger of either breaking down or simply bursting into flames.

For example, on one chilly spring morning, I discovered just how perilous a condition the prehistoric contraptions were in when my journey to the Post Office on trolley bus Number Four was cut short in dramatic style. For most of the way along Peace Avenue, I could smell smoke on board. This was nothing out of the ordinary on any form of Mongolian public transport, so I paid it little heed.

It wasn't until sparks began to appear close to the driver that my attention was piqued. I inched my way forward past two wrinkled old ladies dressed in fur hats and dels (traditional Mongolian overcoats) to get a better view. The driver did not seem the least bit concerned, his foot was to the floor and he was weaving in and out of traffic regardless. By the time we reached the Ulaan Baatar Hotel, however, his demeanour had changed.

The nonchalant driving style had gone and he had begun desperately banging at the dashboard with the clenched fist of one hand and steering with his other. Then, suddenly, we came to an abrupt halt. Everyone waited amidst a sense of hushed anticipation until he managed to prize a panel away from the floor of the bus. A series of bright blue sparks fizzed into the air before a small blaze rose out of the cavity below. Without a word or a hint of surprise, the door was opened, everyone got off and we left the bus smouldering in the street. To put things into even starker context, around a week later, the bus was still by the side of the road happily rusting in the snow.

Cars and buses were only half of Mongolia's environmental problem. Coal-burning accounted for the remaining fumes in the air. The majority of industry around Ulaan Baatar was still coal powered and produced a cloud that drifted depressingly above the capital. It was a point of intense conjecture amongst most expats as to whether the Soviets had intentionally built the majority of UB's factories and power station in a position that caused their fumes to drift across the city, or if it had been a tragic mistake.

On top of these industrial problems, a voracious domestic appetite for coal augmented the pollutants. Central to this voracious coal consumption were UB's Ger districts. The ger is a traditional, nomadic home that Mongolians have used for centuries as their primary form of shelter. They are circular felt tents built around a latticed framework of thin wooden beams and a shallow cone shaped roof. Traditionally, the nomadic Mongolian lifestyle meant that gers were carried on horseback around the steppe and erected whenever and wherever needed. However, in the last century, with the growth of Ulaan Baatar, many Mongolians have moved towards their nation's capital. Large districts made up of shacks and gers now orbit the centre of the city and stretch for miles out towards the countryside.

To keep the interior warm enough to live in, the whole structure of the Ger is built around a large stove at the centre. Because of this design, a ger can be one of the warmest places to spend a harsh Mongolian winter. But, for this to be the case, the occupants need a strong fire in their stove. In more remote areas, herdsmen often use dried wood or animal dung to fuel this. But, in the urban sprawl of the capital city, these were scarce commodities – instead everyone relied upon coal. Each and every ger in the city uses an average of fifteen tons of coal per year. As you might expect, the winter months are easily the worst for pollution. When temperatures plummet, people living in the outlying districts need lots of coal to keep their gers snug and warm. The colder the weather gets, the smoggier Ulaan Baatar becomes.

Along with pollution in the air UB was also afflicted with an environmental problem that was far closer to ground level - rubbish. It was as though a carpet barrage of garbage bombs had hit the entire city. As I have already noted, the first outpost of the refuse kingdom was the stairwell to my apartment. On most days, plastic bags and empty vodka bottles would block half of it, but, on special occasions, there would be bloodied animal bones or even an anonymous rib cage to clutter things even further. However, the rubbish was far from confined to one area - it spread across the city and out into the countryside.

In the winter months, the problem was not a major one, the heavy cold ensured much of the discarded food froze and each fresh grey snowfall kept most of it out of view. It was the arrival of spring and the relative warmth it provided that exacerbated the problem. Once the temperature inched above freezing point, the snow began to melt and expose the level of garbage infiltration. At the same time, much of the disused food and household waste that had been lying on the streets for months on end, began to thaw and take on its own unique aroma.

Overt alcoholism

Pollution was the most conspicuous problem in Ulaan Baatar. Close behind it, however, was drinking. Alcoholism was one of Mongolia's most overt and depressing social crises, and the evidence of its prevalence was in wide-open view. At first, I was shocked by some of the examples of what was fast becoming a national disease. Alas, after a while, the sheer regularity of it all meant that I became anaesthetized against the painful sights on the street.

For example, one cold evening during only my second week in

Bayanzurkh I had finished work and met Fran and Mitch for a beer and dinner. After the meal, I had wrapped up warm and headed down to Peace Avenue to catch my bus home. It was early evening and busy. The bus stop was crowded with people wanting to get home. So, I positioned myself away from the road, out of the wind and waited for either bus number four or thirteen to take me home. The first bus to arrive was a six, which turned off Peace Avenue half a mile or so before Bayanzurkh, so it was no good to me. The majority of the crowd in front of me, though, piled on.

As the passengers all forced their way on board, I looked across and saw a man of around 40 lying motionlessly on the ground. His head was resting on the edge of the pavement as though it were the softest of pillows. He was wearing a coat and hat, and was clutching a bottle containing the last remnants of a litre of vodka to his chest as though it were a sickly infant. I looked around in complete shock. I was asking myself how a man could be in such a condition in such weather. The people remaining at the bus stop did not share my bewilderment. A well dressed middle-aged lady looked down at the inanimate figure then across at me, sniggered and mumbled the word "arkh" – vodka.

Scenes like that were common. However, after my first month, I began to feel a little anaesthetised and they became far less shocking. I quickly developed a degree of apathy and learned simply to step over any inert figures I encountered on the side-walk. This sounds callous, but in reality there was nothing I could do to help them! Bizarre encounters with drunks were an everyday occurrence and, thus, lost much of their shock value. When I would walk to work I was, at first, a touch frightened and simultaneously bemused by the sight of drunks fighting at the gates of Dascholoin Khiid (the monastery situated next door to the MongolNews building). I would take a large detour to avoid any such fracas. By my last few days, however, I was expecting it and was almost disappointed when all I encountered was a monk in his brightly coloured robes.

The reasons behind the growth of the national drink problem are complex. However, it would be logical to identify the Communist regime and its subsequent collapse as the trigger. Prior to the Soviet era, the Russian influence in Mongolia was minimal and a brew known as *airag* was the standard drink of the Mongols. The fermented mare's milk contains only three or four percent alcohol and Mongolians drank it for centuries without developing a dependency or exhibiting such extreme reactions. However, with the Soviets came industry, collectivism, murderous purges and a strong clear spirit. From the 1950s, vodka production in Mongolia grew rapidly. Gradually, consumption in-turn matched this. During the 1960s and 70s, when the Communist system was still capable of providing jobs and homes, alcoholism wasn't a huge problem. When things collapsed, though, Mongolians reached for the bottle.

Just like the other former Soviet satellite states, Mongolia gained both political and economic autonomy in the early 1990s.

Unfortunately, it failed to make the transition to the free market anywhere near as smoothly as countries like the Czech Republic, Poland or Hungary. The economy fell into decline and in the mid 1990s drew to an almost complete halt as Soviet manufacturing, imports and subsidies vanished. It was in the dark heart of the 1990s, as the Democrats struggled to keep control and unemployment began to soar, that alcoholism became institutionalized in the new Mongolia. Industrial production slumped and jobs disappeared. So, many of the male population simply turned to the bottle to deal with the escalating crisis.

The economy has improved in the twenty-first century, but conditions are still not affluent. A Mongolian teacher can expect to take home Tg 50,000 per month, whilst journalists earn around Tg 70,000. Neither of these sums amount to even 50 GBP. Unemployment is also still too high for comfort. Sadly, this means that many Mongolians continue to seek alcohol for solace. With Mongolians still not in a strong enough financial position to escape the national addiction, some alarming statistics persist to this day. For example, according to UN reports 121,000 people out of a population only 2.7 million dramatically overuse alcohol on a regular basis.

The bizarre sights and sobering statistics started to make me think about the Mongolians I lived and worked with, and how deeply alcohol had permeated their lives. Drunkenness in Mongolia was not confined to street corners and gutters. It was also a feature of many households, particularly mine. Batmunkh was a civil servant. From what I could ascertain, that was a relatively well-paid job and a position of responsibility. However, when he came home he enjoyed nothing more than relaxing by cracking open the vodka. There were several occasions when I passed the living room en-route to the kitchen, peaked inside and saw him enjoying a bottle with friends, his wife or sometimes just in blissful isolation. His drinking induced some truly awe-inspiring arguments between himself and Oyuna. Batmunkh was a small, slight man and generally did not offer too much to these exchanges. Oyuna, on the other hand, was short in height but extremely stout in stature and boasted a powerful voice. When she thought her husband had had enough she was not reticent in telling him so - her viewpoint was clear and the windows would often rattle when she enforced it.

Thankfully, none of the people I worked alongside could be included in the alarming figures. Oyun, Uyanga, Sumya, Bulgamaa and Batmunkh all managed to put in a twelve-hour day on a Wednesday with no immediate need to resort to drink. However, each and every week we battled against a midnight deadline, after which the print manager could not guarantee his workers would not have cracked open a bottle and rendered themselves incapable of operating their machinery.

Much of Mongolia's alcohol consumption is gender orientated: Men do the majority of it. Many of the jobs that disappeared with the previous system were industrial and the men who became unemployed often sought alcoholic solace after finding alternative forms of employment scarce. Because of this, women are increasingly filling white-collar jobs in modern Mongolia. The best illustration of this I could find was the media community in Ulaan Baatar where female editor-in-chiefs managed all three English language publications. There was Oyun at the Post and both the Messenger and Montsame had women in charge. Both, coincidentally, were called Indraa.

The alcoholic atmosphere in Ulaan Baatar even had a discernible effect on me. I began to drink far more than I ever would have in England. The first contributory factor to this increase was my work environment where there were no strict office hours and I was free to waltz in at some point in the early afternoon when my hangover had usually receded enough to allow me to edit and write stories. The second factor was the price. Throughout the city, half a litre of Mongolian beer retailed at less than Tg. 2,000 (1 GBP). However, after only a few days we discovered the bar Tse, where the Tg 500 (25p) entrance fee was tempered by the price of a drink being the same amount. It seemed rude not to stop off for a few cold ones, especially as the beer was surprisingly good for such a low price.

However, even though Tse's economic value made it a cheap evening out, it wasn't the major reason we frequented the establishment. Our regular visits were merely designed to alleviate the boredom. Ulaan Baatar may be the coldest and one of the highest capital cities in the world, but it is neither one of the largest nor liveliest. Leisure opportunities were far from plentiful.

It was too cold outside to do any sports or even walk for more than a few blocks. Alongside this, aside from the State Department Store (A large building in the centre of the city that represented most of Mongolia's retail shopping), there weren't too many shops to look around and the only cinemas open showed films in either Mongolian or Russian. My family situation also made it difficult to spend quality time at home. The Batmunkh's lack of English and my inability to speak Mongolian meant I could not sit and chat with Bimba, Azzah or Oyuna. To make things worse the TV channels in the apartment were all in Chinese, Mongolian or Russian. So, what else was there to do? Filling the long, cold winter evenings with something other than local beer became something of a challenge. It was so much of a challenge in fact that we actually had to make concrete plans to avoid the sauce! Our first attempt at sobriety came on a Saturday night in early April ... and fell agonizingly short. We had planned to watch football on Chinese TV in my apartment and simultaneously steer clear of both booze and buuz. In preparation, we visited my local supermarket and stocked up on non-alcoholic goodies like soda, orange juice and hot-dogs. The cost was depressing. The bill for a litre of cola, a carton of orange juice, some sausages and a bag of cookies came to over Tg5,000. A similar amount would have paid for a lavish night in Tse. However, despite the price disparity, our resolve held firm and we settled down to take in an evening of *Holbomborg* (Mongolian for soccer).

Our plan was going well until deep into the first half of the game. Then, without knocking, Batmunkh and Oyuna entered my room carrying a tray with five shot glasses and a large unopened bottle of vodka. Despite our protests we were each forced to take a rather sizable shot. They then scuttled off back to the living room where I can safely presume Batmunkh would have finished what was left in the bottle. If there was one lesson I learned from my three months in Ulaan Baatar and the rest of the country, it was that it is never easy to say 'no' to a Mongolian holding a bottle of vodka and wearing an expectant grin across their face. The Batmunkhs were clearly being hospitable, but it was the last thing we had wanted!

Stray dogs

As malignant as open alcoholism was, it was far from the only noticeable social issue affecting Mongolian society. The stray dogs that roamed the streets of Ulaan Baatar were also far from inconspicuous. Even in England I am not the most devout dog-lover. Anything more than the tiniest sharp-toothed pooch makes me wary and sends me scurrying across the street. With some of the vicious looking animals that lived on the streets of Mongolia's capital city, my little phobia grew by the day. My rabies vaccination had been a major undertaking, but I didn't really want to have to get the benefit from it!

The majority of strays were thin creatures that survived on what they could find in the garbage and from gnawing on discarded animal bones left by the roadside. Their diet and the harsh Mongolian winters meant the creatures were tough and often vicious. During the day, the animals tended to be something of a peripheral sight, hidden away on side streets and alleyways. It was only when darkness fell and the population of the city retreated indoors that the dogs came out and ventured into their element. Once the side-walks emptied of people, the dogs were free to roam and scavenge as they pleased. I always felt particularly uneasy on Wednesday evenings when I would leave the MongolNews building at some point in the early hours. I often saw animals in the shadows and made every possible effort to avoid them.

Even though I managed to avoid stray dogs whilst I was out on the street, it is not inconceivable that I came into contact with them on a completely different and far more disturbing level. Each week Bulgamaa produced a series of snippets that became the UB Post's 'Crime Corner'. I was editing this one chilly Tuesday afternoon when I came across a story that struck me to the bone.

The crux of the piece was the arrest of a group of men who were charged with selling dog carcasses that they had passed off as mutton. This was a perturbing enough story. However, as I read the remainder of the piece I began to feel amazed, disturbed and a little queasy. The most shocking aspect of the whole affair was that some of the meat had found its way onto the tables of one of Ulaan Baatar's public schools. That made for great copy.

However, on a personal level, I was more concerned by the fact that the market in which the meat was sold was in Bayanzurkh. Not only was this close to my house, but, also, it was where Oyuna did her shopping for the entire Batmunkh household. When I began to think of Azzah preparing my food, all that flashed across my mind was the image of her hacking away at an unrecognisable hunk of meat with a large, blood smeared clever. For all I knew it could easily have been mutton or dog.

Homelessness

Stray dogs, alcoholics and excessive quantities of rubbish were all unsightly blemishes on the city. They were indicative of Mongolia's social and organizational problems. Unfortunately, they were also merely the tip of the iceberg. The biggest and most heart-wrenching problem on the streets of Ulaan Baatar was homelessness.

People of all ages were visible living on the street all year round. The most overt figure amongst UB's homeless was a small, outrageously ugly man in his early twenties named Porchilla, who squeezed out a living by begging from foreigners and rich-looking Mongolians. His tactics were to approach at slow pace, almost a stagger, with his palm outstretched and an imploring grimace written across his face. He operated in downtown UB, anywhere from close to the UB Post's offices on Ikh Toiruu, down to and past the State Department Store near Sukhbaatar Square. The expression on his face was almost always too much to ignore.

Whenever I had any small notes in my pocket I would pass them to him so that he could get himself some warm buuz.

Mitch and I tried to get to know Porchilla a little bit and, in so doing, developed a better understanding of life on the street. This all came about one afternoon when Mitch, Ryan (An American I-to-I volunteer at a local boys prison) and I were short of change. We were sitting drinking cans of Mongolian beer in a small park close to the Department Store when Porchilla approached us with his hand in its customary position. None of us had any change to give him - all we had was a spare can of beer. We figured there was nothing else for it, but to offer it to him. I realise this was not helpful to him in the long term, but we figured he would enjoy it. He took it and then, to our surprise, sat right down next to us. He spoke no English, so communication was at best muddled. However, he really tried to get through to us and we were keen to listen.

We managed to find out that to escape the cold he spent his evenings underground in the maze of sewers and heating pipes that run below the city. Apparently, it was the best way for him to keep warm as staying above ground could easily cause you to freeze to death. It was a sobering situation. Once he had finished his beer, he headed off on his way and disappeared below ground. From that point on, it was a touch easier to understand how people survived on the streets, but nigh on impossible to ignore those that did.

Porchilla was not alone in making his home below the streets.

There was also an exceptionally noticeable population of street children. To see them was heartbreaking. Everyday, I would see small scruffy figures scurrying in and out air vents and uncovered manholes. The majority of these appeared between the Post Office and State Department Store on Peace Avenue in the very centre of UB. I don't believe I ever walked along that stretch of the city without being begged for money or food at least once. Over the course of my three months, I saw the children so often that I began to recognize many of them individually. As with Porchilla, this meant refusing them money or looking the other way was almost impossible.

One boy who looked no more than ten or eleven years old was a permanent fixture on the street and never seemed to be more than a block away from the Department Store. He always had in front of him an array of antiquated brushes and worn-out rags that amounted to his shoe shining business. The slight figure was a sobering enough sight on his own. However, the bundle of what appeared to be nothing more than rags that he carried with him made it even worse. Underneath the tattered old clothing was a tiny girl of no more than two years of age, presumably his sister. Whenever I walked past them on a winter afternoon I worried desperately about her freezing to death. During February and early March, I was wearing layer upon layer of thermal clothing and, at times, still felt the cold right through to my bones. It mystified me how the flimsy layers of fabric in which she was wrapped kept her warm enough. I always wore synthetic hiking boots so I never really needed a shoe shine but I would always reach down and drop a few togrogs in his bowl.

Begging and shining shoes were two ways to maintain a bare existence, there were though a variety of others. One of these was to utilize the garbage that engulfed the city. Garbage had grown to be more than just an ugly unrestrained blemish on the Mongolian capital. It had also become something of a cottage industry for those living on the streets. Several children adopted the approach of hunting out disused bottles to sell on to recycling plants. However, whilst this might have made them a few togrogs, it was small scale.

On a more dramatic level, a population of poverty-stricken Mongolians had taken things one-step further. In mid-March, Bulgamaa translated a piece from a Mongolian language newspaper which told the story of a community that had sprung up inside the Ulaanchuluut dumping ground on the outskirts of the capital. The city dump had become a Mecca for those in search of an alternative source of income. Ulaanchuluut's population had risen to over 360 and included many families and children who spent their days sifting through the rubbish in search of bottles and containers that they could sell on to bottling plants. The most prized containers were those of European and American shampoos and cosmetics like L'Oreal and Pantene, for which Ulaan Baatar's bottling plants would pay a higher price because of the greater sell-on value. The plants would then fill them with cheap Chinese shampoo and sell them for a huge mark up. The details of this little scam left me grateful for my own premature hair-loss and slack personal hygiene.

March 8 was Women's Day in Mongolia, a national holiday in honour of the nation's female population. Mongolians celebrate the day by giving the woman of the house flowers and with husbands and children taking over the responsibility of cooking and cleaning for the evening. It was a low-key affair in the Batmunkh household. I had purchased a flower for Oyuna and was prepared to help with making the buuz, but the lady of the house was nowhere to be seen. She had gone out somewhere for the evening and only returned late into the night.

The majority of Mongolians enjoyed Women's Day for the day off work it provided them and the novelty of seeing Mongolian men struggle in the kitchen. The street community, on the other hand, enjoyed it for the money making opportunities it provided. Almost every street kid in Ulaan Baatar had flowers for sale. Where they had got them from was a mystery. With such heavy pollution and the bone-chilling temperatures UB was far from a gardener's paradise. Yet, packs of children hovered by the Department Store and thrust petals and stems into people's faces. Despite the volume of both children and flowers in downtown UB, I purchased mine from a young fellow I encountered on Ikh Toiruu as I walked home. The afternoon of March 8 was, not unexpectedly, bitingly cold. I was making my way back to Bayanzurkh, but was being hindered by a strong headwind. As I crossed an adjoining side street, a boy of about ten appeared out of nowhere. He was dirty, shabbily dressed and carrying a solitary yellow rose. The little guy scurried towards me and held the flower in front of me in an effort to sell it. His eyes were imploring me in a way that few others ever have.

The rose was bright, but slightly pale yellow. The petals were just beginning to show the first signs of wilting and a barely discernible curl was setting in at their tip. At first, I said no. I had planned to stop at my local supermarket and buy one there. However, this little encounter changed my mind. It was not the beauty or the state of the flower that persuaded me to part with a few bills, it was the boy himself. Not only did he look cold and unkempt, but also whilst I was heading back to a warm apartment he was probably bound for a sewer or heating pipe somewhere. I couldn't say no.

Estimates varied dramatically as to how many children either lived permanently on the street or, at the very least, made their living there. The government had the number at a modest 1,500. Various NGOs placed it considerably higher, at between 3,000 and 4,000. They lived in sewers, heating pipes and anywhere else they could find. To feed themselves they collected bottles, sold flowers and shined shoes.

The situation on the street helped me to gain a better insight into my own household. I only knew a few modest details about Azzah and her sister. I had no idea what would have become of them had the Batmunkhs not taken them in, but I dread to think what would have happened had they not. At times, I would see Azzah in the kitchen doing her homework and looking glum. She had every right to. Not only had she lost both her parents, but also she now lived in a crowded apartment where she had little room to study or sleep. However, despite the horrific tribulations that had beset her life, she would often be wearing one of the widest and most infectious smiles in all of Mongolia. It always impressed me that she managed to remain so positive. On the other hand, if the alternatives were as harsh as life on the street, she had every reason to be smiling.

With the problem of such overt homelessness, the debate was raging as to why so many people were without homes and jobs. Much of the issue was related to and tied into that of alcoholism. The economic collapse of the mid-1990s is the key to both problems. The unemployment that drove many adult males to drink also caused a large proportion of older children to quit school in search of income for their family. Whereas 84% of Mongolian children attended primary schools, only 54% were involved in secondary education. The development of alcoholism through the 1990s also began a corrosion of the family structure for many Mongolians. Hundreds of father figures lost any sense of control and their families began to suffer with many becoming violent and abusive. The only escape for their children was to flee to the streets.

We ran a report in the Post that detailed Sukhbaatar district's police department's attempt at reaching some of the children below the streets it patrolled. They escorted a party of journalists from the Mongolian language newspapers down a heating pipe close to the station to see what they would find. Reporters from Onodoor (A Mongolian language paper that was part of the MongolNews group) explained to Bulgamaa how they travelled nearly two kilometres below ground before they encountered any children. The conditions were horrendously unsanitary with the pipes full of dirty water, rats and refuse.

When they eventually came into contact with some children, they were reluctant to speak with either police or journalists. However, those that did, generally revealed that they were escaping difficult family environments. One girl, who was brave enough to speak, told reporters that she left home because of a drunken father who beat her constantly. She had turned to washing and guarding cars for rich businessmen to make enough money for food.

Mongolia's Havel

The picture of Mongolia that this chapter paints is a bleak one. Without doubt the country and its capital have some serious problems that need to be dealt with as quickly as possible. However, the Mongolian people are a strong breed and have emerged into a new world keen to make progress. Their country's problems lie not with them, but with their government in which corruption and inefficiency are lingering Communist hangovers. No elected government has managed to make any kind of inroads into them. Effective reforms would make a massive difference to

UB and its streets, whilst economic improvement would go a long way to cutting alcoholism and homelessness off at their source.

Mongolia has not, as yet, found a leader capable of undertaking the reforms it desperately needs. Its economic crises and inherent disorganization remain unsolved. Until someone steps up and grabs the initiative, the harrowing problems will persist. Many of the countries that freed themselves from Communist tyranny in 1989 and the subsequent years did so with the help of strong and charismatic leaders. Czechoslovakia had Havel, Poland had Lech Walesa and Russia had Boris Yeltsin. Mongolia did have someone who, many Mongolians believe, could also have made a major difference: a small and bespectacled man named Sanjcasurengiin Zorig.

During the pro-democracy movement, Zorig played a key role in helping Mongolia move towards a multi-party democracy. Spurred on by events in Eastern Europe, Zorig organised a series of public protests in Sukhbaatar Square in late 1989. By February of 1990, these had become a fully-fledged reform movement with thousands of supporters. By March, the Communist government had resigned.

The collapse of Communism has its fair share of iconic images: There were Berliners shaking hands through the wall, grizzly footage of the Ceaucescu's being summarily executed and Boris Yeltsin standing on a tank outside Russia's White House. Mongolians would add photos of Zorig sitting on the shoulders of his fellow protesters whilst addressing them with a megaphone.

Once the new political system was in place, Zorig was in the thick of events once more. He was elected to parliament in 1992 and then again in 1996 as a member of the new democratic government. Unfortunately, as discussed earlier, the democratic administration failed to get to grips with Mongolia's mounting problems. Because of this, there was a frighteningly high turnover of prime ministers. Between 1996 and 2000 five men sat in the chair without any great degree of success. After the second of these, Ts Elgbegdorj, was forced to resign because of a banking scandal both the democrats and the MPRP agreed on Zorig as the ideal candidate to step into the breach.

It is impossible to predict whether Zorig would have done any better than the five men who allowed Mongolia to slip into political and economic chaos. Based on what I learned about him, I would like to think he would have. Sadly, though, he never got the opportunity. With the decision to appoint him prime minister made and the announcement to the press prepared, Zorig's life was tragically and brutally cut short.

Returning to his apartment one evening, he found his wife bound and gagged. He was then jumped by a pair of masked assailants who stabbed him repeatedly and hacked at him with an axe. The exact motivations for the killing remain unclear. The prevailing theory amongst most journalists in the country was that he was killed because he had tried to prevent a corrupt casino deal. It was a loss Mongolia still feels to this day.

Postscript*: Many of the problems I outlined in this chapter still persist in Mongolia fifteen years after my trip. In some cases, they have got significantly worse. Chief amongst these is the environment. When I was in UB, coal and petrol made the environment dingy and unappealing. Today, it is not just an aesthetic issue. The coal fumes are now choking the city. According to a 2018 TIME magazine article, in 2016, it overtook Beijing and New Delhi as the world's most polluted capital city. In 2018, UB recorded levels of pollution 133 times higher than the WHO deems safe.*

The alcohol problem is also still a major issue. Mongolia has the world's highest rate of liver cancer and also has the world's highest mortality rate from the disease. The gender issues connected to alcohol also persist. Over the last few years, there have been several newspaper features in international media discussing the rise of women in prominent roles within the country and the problems faced by a generation of men lost to alcoholism. To put things into a sobering context, the gap in life expectancy between men and women is a massive nine years.

4. A WEEKEND AT GRANDPA'S

Less than a month before arriving in Mongolia, I had celebrated the passing of the new year at a party thrown by one of my friends back in England. However, after just a week in Mongolia, I found history repeating itself as I was faced with my second such celebration in the space of just over four weeks. This time, though, it was the lunar version of the holiday.

Most of us in the western world tend to associate this festival with images of colourful dragons and barrages of fireworks in Beijing or Shanghai. The Mongolian version, though, is extremely different. In the Land of the Blue Skies, New Year is known as Tsagaan Sar, which translates roughly to White Months. These festivities have their own unique and far more sombre feel.

During the Communist era, religion was put under intense pressure and ultimately forbidden in Mongolia. In the 1930s, Mongolia faced the same type of purges that Stalin was inflicting across the Soviet Union. Under the leadership of Soviet puppet Khorloohin Choibalsan, Mongolia saw show trials, torture, execution and exile to labour camps. The purges focused on a whole host of 'undesirable' elements. This included the intelligentsia and political dissidents but also Mongolian nationalists, anyone with a pro-Japanese sentiment - this was the time when the Japanese were expanding into Asia and had taken charge of China's northeastern provinces - and Buddhist clergy.

It is estimated that between 20,000 and 30,000 people were executed during the purges, which for a country of Mongolia's size is a big number! Bizarrely, Choibalsan, the architect of the purges, remains relatively visible in Mongolia. Just as with the statue of Lenin, his figure was on show in the capital and his body remained interned in the mausoleum in Sukhbaatar Square that also housed Mongolia's genuine revolutionary hero. There was even a rather dull and industrial city in Mongolia's eastern aimags named after him.

In the 1930s, under Choilbalsan's watch, scores of temples were bulldozed to the ground and the monks who lived within their walls were shot dead or exiled to distant corners of the country. A second part of this religious clampdown was the seemingly permanent cancellation of the traditional Tsagaan Sar holiday. The public celebration of the holiday was banned completely and those celebrating at home could find themselves in serious trouble if they were caught or informed upon by their neighbours. The Communists tried to replace it with a holiday known as 'Collective Herders Day'. Despite the obstacles, many Mongolians still celebrated Tsagaan Sar, but things were extremely clandestine. However, since the collapse of the Soviet-backed regime, it has re-emerged to once more regain its place as a major national celebration.

Absent celebrations

Tsagaan Sar fell on my first full weekend in Mongolia, which meant we weren't fully prepared for it and didn't quite understand what it was all about until it was over. The UB Post closed its offices early on the Friday afternoon, leaving Mitch, Fran and I to gear up for what we thought would be a night on the tiles similar to New Year's celebrations in the west. We began by heading to the British Embassy for our first visit to Steppe Inn. This is the bar that the FCO (Foreign and Commonwealth Office) has built in the grounds of the embassy. It acts as a weekly social club cum networking event cum piss-up for UB's English-speaking expats. After spending the majority of the week holed up in the Post's newsroom with the predominantly Mongolian staff, it was a refreshing change of pace to be amongst the British and members of the Commonwealth again. However, as much as I enjoyed my first English beers in Mongolia and the varied conversation, I was quite keen to get to grips with the Mongolian New Year on a slightly more 'authentic' level.

After bidding our farewell to Steppe, we headed towards Sukhbaatar Square, where I was – quite naively - hoping to find an open-air party along the lines of those in Times and Trafalgar squares. Unfortunately, I was disappointed. As our cab drew us towards the square, all we saw was darkness. The buildings along the perimeter were clearly closed and not even the statue of the famous revolutionary leader in the centre was illuminated. I was disappointed that things appeared to be so quiet. But, when I thought about it, the idea of an open-air party when the temperature was approaching thirty degrees below zero did seem a little foolish. We concluded that everyone must have been celebrating inside somewhere. So, we decided there was nothing else for it but to head for Tse. We naturally assumed the party would be rocking in there.

It was only a five minute walk from the square to Tse which, as we scurried through the snow, we made light work of. However, as we turned the corner we instantly knew that something was wrong when the ever-welcoming yellow light was nowhere to be seen. Tse was closed! This was a horror of epic proportions. Unfortunately, though, it was not alone.

In the entire city, we managed to find just two bars that were open for the holidays. We soon found that these were populated by the same expats we had been chatting and drinking with in Steppe. There was not an actual Mongolian - who was not working in one of the bars - to be found. As our evening ended in something of a damp squib, we trudged off home wondering just what Mongolians did to celebrate their New Year.

White months at home

Only as the Tsagaan Sar weekend drew on did we begin to get a true taste of what a Mongolian New Year was really like. It was all about the family, about buuz and about vodka. Whereas the Batmunkhs spoke no English, Mitch lived in a household where the cousin – Chimgee – spoke it fluently. Because of this, we were invited to their apartment to join their celebrations on the Saturday afternoon. Fran and I arrived just before lunchtime and were straight away thrown into the complex rituals of ceremony and tradition that accompanied the holiday.

After removing our shoes we were led into the main room, where the entire family were seated around a lavishly decorated table. They sat in order of seniority going oldest to youngest in a clockwork direction. Before we could take our seats, we had to greet everyone present. To do this, we had to approach the older guests with our arms outstretched and palms facing upwards. The elder person would then place their hands face down, on top of ours and we would kiss gently on both cheeks. This process was repeated until we reached the people who were younger than ourselves, when our palms were reversed.

Only after this laborious process was complete could we finally sit down and begin to enjoy the special meal. The first course was made-up primarily of what the family called 'white foods'. These were prepared in honour of the arrival of the White Months. There was an array of white candy, some dubious looking dairy products and even sugar lumps. We were told to sample these whilst we waited for the first big course. Just a few moments later, I got a major lump in my throat when I saw possibly the biggest plate of buuz in the history of Mongolia being carried out. I could feel my heart crying out for mercy before I had even tucked into the first of what would inevitably be many!

Before we could begin to eat, though, we had to go through a series of ceremonial toasts. These began with the most senior male present. In our case, this was Chimgee's great-uncle who stood up and set off on what seemed to be a very long and winding speech. Everything he said in his toast was in Mongolian and we understood nothing. However, it was clear that we were meant to acknowledge what he said. Therefore, at regular intervals throughout the speech, the old man would stop, lift his glass and drain it at pace – the only thing we could do was to follow suit. When he finally finished we were instructed to eat the buuz.

The combination of mutton fat and vodka did not sit well in my stomach. As I sat, struggling to digest the heavy mix, an old lady – her exact position in Chimgee's family was not particularly clear - got up and declared that it was time for a song. We figured this wasn't a bad idea and settled back to hear some traditional Mongolian folk tunes. The first was sung by one of the older men and his son, a strapping fellow of maybe only five and a half feet in height but with an imposingly squat frame. The old man sang with a shrill, high-pitched tone, which the son off set wonderfully with a booming tenor style voice. We were impressed with the song and gave a hearty round of applause when they had finished. It was only as our clapping tailed off that we noticed everyone in the room looking at us.

To our horror, we discovered that the singing was a participatory event. The three of us looked at each other blankly. We had absolutely no idea what to sing. We discussed the possibility of reciting Auld Lang Syne to fit in with the New Year motif, but were forced to shelve the idea when we realized none of us actually knew more than the opening lines. After debating what we could sing for almost five minutes, we had to settle for Ba Black Sheep – it was pretty much the only thing we all knew the words to.

We began the little ditty confidently enough and even appeared to be getting a relatively good reception, until ... we forgot the words and ground to a halt. There was then an uncomfortable silence before we managed to mumble our way to the end with a few improvised words. The Mongolians gave us a polite round of applause and then motioned for us to drink some more. We needed it!

Tsagaan Sar at the Batmunkhs

The afternoon at Mitch's apartment was both interesting and entertaining. We left early in the evening feeling just a little worse for wear – an afternoon of buuz and vodka will do that to you! As I took the bus home along Peace Avenue, I quickly began to notice that I was not the only one who had been enjoying a little Tsagaan Sar drink. On the seat opposite mine was a well-built man who looked to be in his early thirties and who seemed to be another example of Mongolia's issues with alcohol. He was slumped forward with his head resting on the seat in front.

81

The bus was lurching and jerking forward, and braking sharply each time it was cut up by a car or taxi. Yet, no matter how uncomfortable the journey was, the man remained motionless. If it weren't for a brief moment when he regained consciousness enough to sneeze, I may have begun to worry that he was dead. When I got off at the bottom of Sansar he was still firmly comatose and in serious danger of missing his stop, if he had not already.

I ambled along a very cold Sansar before arriving home and collapsing on my bed to sleep off the vodka and buuz. Unfortunately, my slumber was cut short after only a few minutes when there was a firm bang on my door. Before I had the chance to answer, in walked Batmunkh and Oyuna carrying a tray, a large bottle of vodka and three bowl-like shot glasses.

The absolute last thing I was in the mood for was more vodka, although I did take consolation in the fact that a plate of steaming buuz didn't accompany it. Oyuna folded out my small table, placing the tray on top of it before Batmunkh began to pour. Much to my disappointment, he was in a generous holiday mood and was filling each glass right to the brim. He handed his wife a glass and then did the same for me. They both raised them, proclaimed "Tsa!" (Cheers) and deposited the contents with very little fuss. I had no choice but to attempt to follow suit. Somehow, I managed to force it down. With the first glass still burning on the way down Oyuna stepped out of the room, leaving Batmunkh and I to 'enjoy' the rest of the bottle together –

we were to share no words, just the vodka.

The man of the house was wearing a sly little grin across his face as he sat enjoying his favourite pastime with the mysterious new house-guest. He poured the vodka again and handed me a glass as full as the previous one. I was aware that custom dictated that if I were only to take sip of this second one, Batmunkh would see that I had had enough and would take no offence. However, I had spoken very little to Batmunkh and deeply wanted to develop something of a relationship with my host. So, to his great delight, I took a massive gulp and sank the drink. He laughed and clapped his hands, clearly seeing the pain written across my face. Whilst I sat wincing, he drained the remainder of the bottle into our glasses and got up to leave. As he passed through the door, he wore a wide grin and offered me one final "Tsa!"

I never really managed to develop much of an open understanding with Batmunkh. In fact, the little holiday interlude was the closest we ever got to a meaningful conversation. However, after that point, whenever I came home showing the effects of a night in Tse or Steppe, Batmunkh would offer me the same wry grin as he did when we were drinking vodka together and I would laugh in reciprocation.

Off to Grandpa's

I woke up with a slight headache on the Sunday. The prospect of more vodka and more buuz did not seem the most appealing. However, Chimgee had invited us to go with her to visit her grandfather, who lived in a ger on the outskirts of the city. Therefore, the chances of seeing more of both weren't slim. I met her and Mitch at around eleven to take the bus out there. Just as on my trip home the previous night, there were plenty of examples of Mongolian alcoholism on show as we saw several men slumped against their wives or the seats in front of them. At that time of day, it was difficult to tell whether they were exhibiting the after-effects of the night before, or they had already made a start that morning. Neither option painted things in a great light!

The bus bumped and weaved along Peace Avenue before turning off and heading away from the city centre. It didn't take too long for the buildings by the roadside to give way to a vast collection of shacks and gers. Then, after a further fifteen minutes driving, the bus stopped. Chimgee told us to get off and pointed up a dirt track where her grandfather's home was.

I was very keen to go with Chimgee and Mitch in order to see a real-life ger and I also wanted to see the ger districts. Until that point, all I knew of those areas was what I had read and edited at the Post. I knew they were a huge source of pollution, I knew they were an area with a very high level of poverty and I also knew that they weren't the safest area in UB. On a Sunday morning they didn't seem to be too dangerous but they did have a very ramshackle feel to them. There were no paved roads; the only way to get around was along frozen dirt tracks. Nothing in the districts was permanent. People either lived in gers or wooden shacks. It really didn't look affluent.

From the bus stop, we walked about thirty meters up the track before Chimgee opened a gate in a high wooden fence and we entered a small yard containing a lot of snow, a small outhouse and a solitary ger. To enter, we were forced to crouch down in order to fit through the doorway that measured barely four feet in height. Once inside, we could extend ourselves a little once more, but still couldn't stand up straight. It seemed to be a little bigger than it appeared outside, but was not what you would call spacious. The interior was pretty gloomy. The only window in the place was at the top of the cone shaped roof where the pipe from the stove poked through. The whole ger was illuminated by just two light bulbs, so it took a few seconds for my eyes to adjust to the light inside. When they did, I could see that at the centre of the circular structure was a stove and small table. Around the outside were three beds – that doubled as couches - and two brightly decorated chests. On two of the beds were seated Chimgee's uncle and his family, whilst at the far end sat her grandfather and grandmother. They were both wearing dels and both had short gray hair.

Again, we had to embark on the ritual greetings with our hands out-stretched to meet theirs. After we had kissed them on the cheek, we all sat to enjoy some more white foods. Just as the previous day, there was candy, sugar lumps and various dairy products for us to nibble on before the buuz came out. This time, however, there was an exciting new addition to the menu – airag.

This was mare's milk that had been set aside for three months and allowed to ferment, giving it a slightly fruity taste and an alcoholic kick of similar strength to a glass of beer. Grandma served us a glass that was taken straight out of a large churn at the side of the stove. At first, the bizarre taste had me wincing a little with each sip, but after a while I began to develop a taste for it and it started to sink a whole lot easier. It certainly did not match a pint of Chinggis Khan beer, but it was not bad at all.

With the airag slipping down with relative ease, Chimgee's grandfather decided it was time for a toast. Up until that point, he had been pretty quiet and had not really joined the conversation. However, when he picked up a shot glass and began a series of toasts, things changed dramatically as he took on a whole new persona. Despite speaking no English, he was desperately keen to communicate with his new guests and directed all his speeches at Mitch and I.

His first toast was a short one welcoming us to his home, which we all followed by sinking our drinks. The glasses were quickly refilled before he made another very similar one. He then jumped in with a toast to international friendship and solidarity and one offering us his hospitality. In the space of five minutes he had welcomed us and expressed his friendship with seven different but eerily similar toasts. With each stinging hit of cheap vodka, it became clear that he was enjoying the drinking as much as the actual welcoming.

Once the toasts had finished, the buuz continued to be served in quantities as frighteningly large as the previous day. We sat and ate them slowly, whilst simultaneously allowing the heavy burning caused by drinking so much vodka in such a short period of time to ease. As we sat and chatted with Chimgee, Grandpa got up and came to sit next to us, and attempted to strike up a conversation in Mongolian. Naturally, we looked at him blankly as we didn't have the slightest clue as to what he was talking about Nonetheless, we nodded our heads in approval. Chimgee then interjected apologetically to explain that he had been drinking all morning and was now in a state of pretty severe intoxication and even she wasn't exactly sure what he was talking about. Nevertheless, she translated his questions as best she could for us to answer.

We explained to him that I was from England, Mitch was from Canada and that we were both in Mongolia working as journalists. He seemed delighted to learn this and proffered toasts to Canada, to England and to journalists. Around three minutes later, we explained the same things again as, because of his drunkenness, he had already forgotten. Chimgee continued to offer apologies for him, but we laughed them off as we were enjoying the novelty of hanging out with a riotously drunk octogenarian Mongolian.

Lunch at Grandpa's was proving to be supremely entertaining as he continued to instigate bizarre and broken conversation and offer some dramatic toasts. However, things took a bit of a dip when he decided it was time for a song. With the day before and our hideous failure still fresh in our minds, Mitch and I looked at each other with a sense of fear about the prospect of going through it all again. But, first we had to listen to Grandpa. Through Chimgee's translation he informed us that he was going to sing a traditional Mongolian folk song. He then then began by making an almost indescribable shrieking noise. We hoped that maybe he was just loosening up the vocal cords and the real song would commence in a few seconds. Unfortunately, we had no such luck. For around five minutes, he warbled his way through something that I wouldn't really describe as a song. As he did so, we looked around the room to see his family, almost in unison, shaking their heads and rolling their eyes. We were glad that it was not just us who couldn't stand the din!

With such a precedent set, even we couldn't embarrass ourselves when our turn came ... surely. This time, instead of a combined effort Grandpa wanted to hear a number from each of us. This gave me a sickening feeling in the pit of my stomach, since my vocal efforts are generally nothing other than terrible. The one saving grace was that I could choose a song where I knew all the words. I opted for a folk song I had learned in America and Mitch went for a Canadian rock song of which he knew two or three verses. Thankfully, we both managed to remember the words and our lack of tune was somewhat overlooked as we each received a hearty round of applause. Our reward for the less than harmonious efforts was another shot of vodka from Grandpa.

By the time the songs and the accompanying shots of vodka were both finished, we had joined Grandpa in the ranks of the drunks.

The three of us were all seated together doing lots of talking, but not really saying all that much. Grandpa repeatedly welcomed us to Mongolia and we repeatedly thanked him and told him how nice it was of him to invite us to his home. Each of these little interludes was greeted by a shot of vodka.

Amidst the mist of buuz, vodka and garbled semi-translated conversation, Grandpa suddenly found a moment of clarity, reached up into the roof and pulled down a book of Buddhist writings. He began reading from them. Although we didn't understand what he said, we listened intently to what was clearly a very spiritual moment. For a brief period after he finished, we all sat there silently. Chimgee whispered to us that he had been saying a prayer for the family's departed relatives. It was all very moving.

The silence was broken only when the old man took a closer look at my head and noticed that it was almost bereft of hair and was, therefore, very similar to the many Buddhist monks around UB. Once this realization dawned on him, he shouted out: "Buddha" and then slapped me on the top of the head with his book.

Everyone around us laughed vociferously at Grandpa's little outburst, but it was becoming clear that Grandpa had had enough to drink and maybe we ought to make tracks. Chimgee suggested this to her Grandfather who was less than enthused with the idea – he was having way too much fun with his new drinking buddies. Five minutes of arguing did appear to have brought a compromise when Grandpa agreed with the rest of the family that it would be ok if we stayed for one more vodka then left. However, this compromise ran aground when it became clear there had been something of a communication shortfall. Where Chimgee had meant one shot of vodka, Grandpa had been thinking of another bottle. At that point, everyone decided enough was enough and we were shepherded back out into the cold and home to sleep off New Year.

5. HUNGRY LIKE THE WOLF

By the end of February, our explorations of Mongolia were still limited to the smoggy and frozen confines of Ulaan Baatar. We desperately wanted to visit the vast tracts of grassland, mountainous peaks and wind-swept deserts that for which Mongolia is renowned. However, with the snow and ice still entrenched on the streets of the capital and temperatures across much of the country still below −20, we had few options and were beginning to go a bit stir crazy stuck in the city. Ulaan Baatar had become something of an ice-prison. Mongolia's lack of transport options also hindered our hopes of some pleasant sightseeing jaunts. The railway line ran only from north to south and, instead of roads, the majority of the country was served by dirt tracks that, in the winter, were not easily passable. In short, we were looking to break out, but were scant on any sort of cunning plan. Thankfully, Chimgee offered us the safest and most attractive option of escape. Her uncle – who owned a rather powerful 4X4 that he used for tourist excursions - would drive us to the northern city of Darkhan for the weekend. We could stay in her mother's apartment whilst she was away in China and from there, we could head out onto the steppe and spend a day with her grandfather (Her other Grandfather) who, apparently, was one of the region's best hunters - he would, she assured us, be stone cold sober. We discussed the proposition amongst ourselves and decided that a trip onto the steppe would be an excellent cure for the cabin fever that was beginning to set in.

So, after a heavy Friday night at Tse, we woke Saturday morning and gingerly climbed into Yamcah's (Chimgee's Uncle) four-wheel-drive jeep, ready for a trip that would take approximately four hours. The road north was a thin sliver of tarmac that bisected hundreds of miles of unbroken, unspoiled snow. It was barely two lanes wide with the snow on either side spilling over and forming little banks of ice. Whenever we encountered anything coming the other way we both had to slow down to a crawl and inch past each other with both vehicles being forced to drive with two tires on the road and other two in the ice and snow. However, regardless of the slow and at times precarious progress, the journey to Darkhan was enjoyable for the crisp, clean white snow and bright blue skies. It was a refreshing change from Ulaan Baatar and the covering of smog and dingy coal stained snow. After a month in Mongolia, we were finally getting to see the much-vaunted scenery and it was easy to understand why the country was labelled the 'land of the blue skies'.

The pristine conditions changed very quickly once we got within sight of Darkhan. Just as in UB, there was a smoggy cloud hanging over the city and the snow was beginning to take on an all too familiar grayish tinge. Darkhan is Mongolia's second city and a major industrial centre. The relatively new 'metropolis' was built in 1961 with not inconsiderable assistance from Moscow. The Soviets provided Mongolia with top planners and architects from every corner of the Eastern bloc, who managed to create a city where once there had been just wilderness. It is only 100 kilometres from the Russian border, which meant it was in an ideal location for industry that could be serviced by supplies and technology from all across the eastern bloc. Because of this, the city grew up around a series of joint industrial ventures between Mongolia and other Socialist countries.

The problem today is that, like most of Mongolia, Darkhan is suffering from a Socialist hangover. The majority of the industry has closed and the city appears cold, dejected and deserted. Darkhan is home to over 60,000 Mongolians, but as we drove through the outskirts towards Chimgee's mother's apartment, the streets were empty and the city seemed eerily quiet.

A day in Darkhan

Our first port-of-call was the town's museum. The institution was housed in three slightly grubby rooms above a convenience store but, despite its inauspicious location, it housed some really interesting exhibits. One room was full of traditional Mongolian artifacts such as a full size ger and an array of traditional clothing. Although those exhibits were quite interesting, it was one of the other rooms that captured my attention. It contained displays on the history of the city and featured a large, glass-cased model of how it was designed to look when it was first constructed. It was interesting to compare the designs with what we had already seen. The overall layout of the city remained, but much of the industry that was shown in the model was now long since derelict.

As interesting as the exhibits were, it took barely forty-five minutes to peruse the museum in its entirety. The next stage of our tour was a trip out to the hills that surround the city. We drove out of Darkhan and off the road to the peak of a small hill. From there, we could see across the town and out onto the steppe beyond, which looked beautiful under the blanket of heavy snow. Darkhan, unfortunately, looked nothing more than a dirty stain.

After a few minutes up on the hill, the wind began to bite and we decided it was time to get back into town, pick up some supplies, then get settled into the apartment. To this end, we headed for Darkhan's main supermarket, which was housed in what was formerly the Worker's Palace. Above the entrance was the second statue of Lenin we had seen. He was striking the sort of pose that suggested he was leading the workers onward towards revolution. It was a strange contradiction and probably epitomised the paradox of modern Mongolia with capitalism sat in the heart of the former Communist infrastructure.

I am not too sure Lenin would have enjoyed seeing a Communist institution selling American sodas and Korean candy. As poignant as the place appeared, though, we were not too concerned about its symbolism. It was well stocked with noodles, beer and cereals. So, we filled our baskets and headed for the jeep.

Darkhan's Worker's Palace was actually quite similar to its counterpart in Ulaan Baatar. The capital city's version was slightly larger, but had also been severed from its Socialist past. UB's Palace had not been transformed into a supermarket, but rather one of the best pool halls in Mongolia. Fran and I spent several afternoons crashing the balls around the table and filling time before work. It was a bizarre place to shoot pool. Despite its new vocation it still retained much of its old identity and included a giant bust of Lenin that stood above the refreshments counter watching each ball being potted.

Buddha is back

With our supplies in the back of Yamcah's 4 x 4, we headed for the apartment. Our plan was to take a rest before going for dinner and then visiting a newly erected statue of Buddha. We ate Chinese food at a surprisingly well-stocked restaurant. Some sweet and sour chicken and noodles was a hugely welcome change from the incessant buuz in UB. We then headed into the night to visit the landmark.

The seated figure of Buddha was over thirty feet tall and twenty feet in diameter. We had noticed it on our way into Darkhan, but had paid little attention. In the daytime, the white stone barely stood out against the snow and blended into the local panorama. At night, when the statue was illuminated, it was a different story. The clear, darkened sky was the perfect backdrop and the white stone reflected light like some giant, slightly ghostly beacon.

The scale of the new Buddha told a great deal about Buddhism in Mongolia, for which the last century was not a good one. It may have begun with imperial China in control of the country and Buddhism being allowed to flourish, but it would take less than 30 years for things to change dramatically. 1924 and independence from China should have been a new dawn for the country. However, it didn't take long for the independence that had been 300 years in coming to become nothing more than a token as Communism tool root. Sadly. Buddhism bore the brunt of Choibalsan and his purges.

Of the 27,000 Mongolians who lost their lives to the purges, half were Buddhist monks. With the majority of Mongolian Buddhism's senior figures disappearing, so too did their temples and monasteries as Choibalsan made serious efforts to remove every sign of the religion from Mongolia. The only Buddhist building left standing was Gandan Khiid in UB, which was allowed to stand as some kind of symbolic reminder. Taking such historical precedent into account, the statue was clearly not just a depiction of the religious figure, it was also a celebration of the new tolerance in the country. For sixty years, Buddhism had been driven underground. Now. it was part of Mongolian culture once more and there were many Mongolians keen to celebrate that fact.

After visiting the statue, we made our way back to the apartment to get some much-needed shut-eye. We would be starting the following day very early. Chimgee's grandfather wanted to be out on the step by first light, so we needed to be up before five-thirty.

Trailing the wolf

We were up very early and we soon discovered that northern Mongolia in the dead of night was very dark and extremely cold. We wrapped ourselves up very very warm and squeezed into the back of the 4x4. We made our way out of the city in the direction of the ger districts which, like in UB, ringed the city. Just as with Chimgee's other grandparents, hunting Grandpa had a traditional Mongolian abode. He lived in an old wooden cabin.

To get there, we drove past the ghostly figure of Buddha and out of town. The 'road' into the ger district was bump, very bumpy. I was still desperately tired and was making every effort possible to catch a few winks of sleep in the back seat. However, transport in Mongolia is rarely conducive to this and I was constantly prevented from drifting off by my head crashing against either the window or the roof. This was a pattern that would become familiar during the course of my stay in Mongolia and would ensure I was awake to enjoy almost every minute of my travels across the country.

After twenty minutes bouncing along the snow-covered dirt track, we arrived outside a small wooden cabin from which a short, wrinkled, old man emerged. He was carrying a small bag, some binoculars and two long shotguns. The jeep was already quite full with Yamcah driving, Mitch in the passenger seat and Fran, Chimgee and I in the back seat. When Grandpa arrived he had to take the prime position in the front, relegating Mitch to the back, which suddenly became a very cramped locale. The best option to relieve this was for someone to jump into the trunk alongside the guns and ammunition. We opted to rotate the responsibility between the three of us with me going in first.

The boot wasn't as uncomfortable as I first imagined. I wedged myself into a corner and managed to avoid being flung against the roof and walls. The only problem was the darkness. Yamcah could only see as far his headlights penetrated. This meant that he got very little advanced warning of rocks and troughs. So, occasionally, we would dramatically lurch forward or from side-to-side sending me hurtling across the width of the jeep with my legs flailing in the air.

Aside from the headlights, the only other hint of light we encountered in the dense early morning sky came thirty minutes into our expedition when Grandpa caught a fleeting glimpse of two small, red-eyes off to our left. Yamcah pulled the jeep to a slow halt and killed the engine. I passed Grandpa his shotgun - which had been stowed in the boot next to me - and we waited. The barrel was pointed out through the passenger window whilst

Grandpa peered out into the night in search of the eyes. The tension was palpable. Until that point, our hunting trip had felt like a silly jaunt. But, suddenly, things began to feel very real. After five minutes of still silence, though, the cold began to creep through the open window and there was still no sign of the small red dots. The old man sighed and drew the weapon back inside the vehicle - a small animal had just had a very close escape.

Once the gun was safely stowed back beside me, Yamcah started the engine and we continued to plough into the night. In the early morning darkness, it was difficult to gauge in which direction we were heading - all our bearings had been completely removed in the all-encompassing blackness. We finally ascertained that Yamcah was taking us west when the sun began to rise and the first few delicate shrouds of light reflected through the rear window. It was still a long way to the hunting ground, so I contented myself by watching the sunrise behind us.

The transition from darkness to light was stunning. The sky went from black, through a series of deep dark blues before finally emerging as brilliant, bright and cloudless. It was almost nine when we reached Grandpa's favoured hunting area. We drew up on a small, snowy outcrop where a second jeep was parked. The old man and Yamcah disembarked so as to speak with the del covered occupants.

Up until that point, we didn't really know what kind of animals Grandpa had in mind for our hunt. Before we left UB, Chimgee had told us she figured he might have his eyes on birds or small mammals that might be braving the winter snow. However, Grandpa had got some quality inside information from his buddies. So, our plans were about to change. When he got back into the car, he said something in Mongolian and Chimgee let out an excited "Oooh". Apparently, Grandpa's friends had spotted a pack of wolves in the area. So, our prey had changed and things were suddenly a lot more exciting.

The prospect of hunting wolves was a conflicting one. Let's be clear, I would be massively skirting the truth if I claimed that the prospect of hunting them across the frozen steppe was anything other than utterly thrilling. It totally captured my imagination and was the type of activity that I was hoping to find when I booked my flights to Mongolia. However, I am no hunter and the thought of killing such a large and majestic animal did not sit well. For me, it would just be wrong. I was pretty sure that were I given the opportunity to fire the gun, I would be left wanting. Out on the frozen steppe, I was a tourist and I didn't want to have a negative impact on the environment I was visiting. However, Grandpa was not chasing wolves for fun and that made things more complex.

In the northern reaches of Mongolia snaring a wolf can be tremendously valuable for any huntsman. The meat is said to have intrinsic medicinal values and is widely sought by herdsmen and their families. The fur is also a precious, saleable commodity in both Mongolia and over the Russian border to the north. I concluded that I would have less concern - although not zero concern - if Grandpa were the man who pulled the trigger and put the animal to good use. He would be hunting for his livelihood, whilst we would have been hunting for something that could maybe be described as 'sport'. Also, in all seriousness, the chances of me actually being able to get anywhere close to hitting a moving animal with an old Soviet rifle were pretty much nonexistent.

The wolf also holds a special, spiritual position in Mongolian life. Many Mongolians believe that Chinggis Khan was descended from the union of a deer and a wolf, and that Mongolian society has evolved from these animals. Men supposedly take their influence from the wolf, whilst the deer influences women. A reflection of this is the national crest, which is winged by a deer on one side and a wolf on the other - the UB Post's sky blue banner featured this very crest in the centre. As the wolf holds such a vaunted position, hunting and killing one is considered a significant feat. The animal's craft and guile are said to be its most valued characteristics and the huntsman who claims the beast's life inherits those traits from it.

The major species of wolf on the steppe is the gray wolf. These beasts can reach two-to-three feet in height and up to six feet in length. However, despite being such a valuable prey, the wolf is on the rise in Mongolia. This has been caused primarily by the collapse of the Communist system, under which large-scale twice-annual wolf hunts were organized and approaching 5,000 wolves a year were killed. Since these hunts have stopped, the animals have begun to flourish. They have also been the beneficiaries of Mongolian herding practices. The traditional herdsmen are loathed to feed and water their animals over the long, cold winter months - survival is hard enough for humans without factoring animals into the equation. Consequently, they allow many of their animals to roam the steppe for half the year and find their own food. This ensures there is plentiful supply for the hungry wolves. After our little stop, with our pulses racing and adrenaline pumping, the jeep pulled away and we went in search of the much-vaunted wolves. Prior to the trip, Chimgee had told us that her grandfather was seen by many in the area as the best hunter in all of Darkhan. As he was so good, as we set off on the trail, she assured us that we could probably expect to at least sight some wolves even if we didn't bag one of the animals. Her claims appeared to be well-founded when, after less than half-an-hour's driving, Grandpa signalled to stop the jeep. He quickly got out and examined some tracks he had spotted in the snow. He ascertained they were made by the wolves we were searching for. He jumped back in and we set off following the trail. Only a few minutes later Yamcah brought us to a halt again. Grandpa had his binoculars against his face and had sighted a pack of three wolves. We each stared through the eyeglasses with fascination. The wolves were a long way off and looked tiny against the sweeping scenery. But, nonetheless, they looked magnificent and seeing them out in their natural habitat was one of the greatest things I had ever seen. We could admire them for only so long, though, before Grandpa signalled for us to move off and begin the chase. The wolves were on a hillside across a small valley. The distance between us and them was approaching half-a-mile, so they had a good head start on us. Yamcah revved the jeep and we were away. Unfortunately, our engine may well have been our downfall. As soon as Yamcah touched the gas our prey pricked up their ears, took to their heels and disappeared out of view before we had even travelled a hundred meters. This was no major obstacle for our wise old guide, though. He had found the animals using their tracks and he could follow them the exact same way.

Now that we were in pursuit, Yamcah was far less cautious in his driving style. Where he had previously negotiated the rolling, snow covered hills gingerly and at a very low speed, he was suddenly taking a more carefree approach. Every inch of the jeep's chassis and bodywork was rattling as we made our way down the hillside and onto the opposing slope. In the boot, I was bouncing around chaotically like I was on a rollercoaster and my head was banging against the windows and roof. Mercifully for my newly acquired headache, we stopped briefly for Grandpa to check the tracks before making our way over the crest of the hill and down into a second sweeping valley. To our dismay, the wolves were nowhere to be seen. However, the trail was still hot and Grandpa pointed us in the direction of their tracks.

The experience was gripping. At any point, the animals could have been over the crest of the next hill or could have appeared from behind the next snowy twist of the steppe. The driving was also thrilling. With Yamcah adopting his laissez-faire approach to navigating the difficult terrain, we were bouncing and lurching from side-to-side and front-to-rear like a wild and perpetual fairground attraction. Sadly, despite Grandpa and Yamcah's best efforts, we could not keep up with the wolves.

The trail, finally, went cold when we met a series of large rocky outcrops. The tracks through the snow that had kept us within striking distance of our prey suddenly disappeared and we were relying on nothing more than Grandpa's instincts. His first tactic in searching out the wolves was to get as high possible to find a panoramic vantage point. To do this, Yamcah pointed the jeep up an almost vertical hillside and with a spin of his wheels began our ascent. The others were thrown back in their seats and I was thrown back against the rear window. Once at the top the view was again spectacular. However, it did not contain any wolves. Grandpa got out with his binoculars to scour the horizon in every direction. Alas, we were out-of-luck, the wolves had made a clean break of it.

To console ourselves, we decided to take an early lunch. Chimgee had packed us horse-meat sandwiches and a bizarre snack comprising horse steak stuffed into the horse's own intestine. It was greasy fare. However, outside the temperature was many degrees below freezing and the wind was sending it plummeting even further. After a few hearty bites, I quickly understood why the meat was popular with locals. Eating it regularly would surely be an excellent way of helping the body deal with the bitter cold and it helped me feel a little more revived.

Once we had polished off the snacks, Grandpa decided to cut his losses in the search for wolf. The plan was now to head back home picking up any animals we could find on the way. Chimgee explained that there might be some birds or rabbits around. It seemed, though, that our luck was a long way out as all the other animals proved to be as elusive as the wolf. This ensured we crept back to Darkhan with empty handed and with our tails firmly between our legs.

Back in the city centre, it was only two in the afternoon, but we were exhausted. We had been up since five and had travelled through the darkness into the frozen wilderness and then back again. So, it was time for a snooze. After our morning escapades, the afternoon and evening most certainly failed to compare. We ate dinner and played cards before we hit the sack. It was another early start in the morning. We had the town monastery to visit before making the journey back to UB as I had to be in the office later that afternoon.

The monastery was another indicator as to just how hard Choibalhsan's purges had hit Mongolian Buddhism. It was made up of three buildings and a series of covered prayer wheels. The largest of the buildings was adorned with a small plaque in Cyrillic script that, although linguistically incomprehensible to us, disclosed the dates 1932 and 1991. A translation was not required to explain what they meant.

6. THE GODFATHER OF MONGOLIAN ROCK

For my first couple of weeks in Mongolia, I spent the majority of my working time in the newsroom editing stories and helping with page design. This was great fun, but, after a while, I began to get a craving to get down to some reporting of my own. Oyun gave me the chance to do just this when she asked me to review a concert by the top Mongolian hip-hop act – Ice Top. The band was doing a series of shows over three nights at the UB Palace in downtown Ulaan Baatar. So, I went along with Mitch and Fran to take in some modern Mogolian music.

The Palace was originally built during the Communist era, so it had a familiarly brutish exterior, but it had been re-developed along western lines in the mid 1990s. It contained the genuinely terrible disco club Laser Land, two other bars and a clean, modern auditorium. I arrived for the gig slightly before Mitch and Fran, so I was forced to wait in the foyer and familiarize myself with some of my fellow concert-goers. The place was awash with teenage Mongolians dressed in their finest baggy clothing and baseball caps.

Aside from the occasional over-protective mother, bartender or ticket vendor, at 24 I was by far and away the oldest person in the building. I found it remarkable that so many young people had showed up to the event considering the ticket price was Tg5,000. This was a hefty amount for a country where the average wage was only around Tg50,000 per month. I figured that for such a big price tag, I would be in for a treat. I was wrong! Really wrong! Once we got into the event, the auditorium was full to bursting and no one appeared to be paying the least bit of attention to his or her assigned seat numbers. So, feeling conspicuously old and conspicuously non-Mongolian, we opted for a low-key position away from the throng. We were off to the left, but still close enough to the stage to satisfy our journalistic curiosity. The opening acts were far from inspiring. Hardly any appeared to be above fifteen years of age and even fewer of them could actually sing. However, they were making a valiant effort and were throwing in some badly choreographed dance moves for good measure. The vast throng of teenage Mongolians didn't look particularly interested either and merely clapped politely as each successive act trudged off stage.

When the star attraction took the stage, the atmosphere changed completely. Everything went dark and pounding drum beats began to fill the room as eight brightly dressed young men burst onto the stage from all corners. It was like a weird hip-hop rainbow. They looked pretty weird to us, but the rest of the crowd got very excited very quickly. The unrestrained demeanours disappeared and were replaced with frantic waving and screaming. It was a reaction like that to the Beatles at Shea Stadium, only it was Northern Asia and the band was garbage. Whilst the rest of the crowd were working themselves into a frenzy, the three of us were staring at each other blankly. We really weren't sure what all the fuss was about.

After four or five very similar sounding songs the crowd was still enraptured, and Mitch, Fran and I were still at a loss as to why. Before coming to the concert, Batmunkh had given me a bit of a heads up about Ice-Top. Apparently, they had been heralded as a new dawn in Mongolian music because they combined external musical styles with their native language, which was something young people in Mongolia believed was pretty unique. In fairness to them, they had clearly managed this important achievement. However, the major musical and stylistic problem they faced ... was that they were rubbish. It seemed they had found tunes that would have appalled some of the western world's most hideous boy bands, added some garish track suits and jumped out in front of hundreds of young people who knew no better or had no other option but to like them. It wasn't like Eminem and other big hip-hop acts were holding gigs in UB.

The eight members of the band managed to break dance and shimmy their way through well over an hour of bland tunes, which despite their lack of both edge and quality had the audience transfixed. At that point, we decided enough was enough and shuffled out of the auditorium and into the biting cold to find our way home.

Ready to rock

The UB Post went to press the following Wednesday featuring approximately 270 words on Ice-Top's performance - not many, in fact very few, of them were entirely positive. However, I had barely finished my scathing attacks when Oyun suggested I review a second Mongolian band. This time it would be the veteran rockers Kharanga. With Sunday's precedent in mind, I was not keen, but found myself persuaded to make my way to the UB Palace once more.

Whereas Ice-Top drew a massive crowd of teenagers and three rather unimpressed western journalists, Kharanga attracted a far more varied clientele. There were locals of all ages and more than just the three of us from outside Mongolia's frozen borders. However, despite the increased diversity, attendance was sparse and the crowd was far less than the one that witnessed the previous week's hip-hop 'extravaganza'. Yet, even though the auditorium was barely half full, the show was far more entertaining and had us in our seats until the very last chord had been played.

We were late into the gig having been let down by UB's unreliable public transport, but were greeted by powerful guitar music from an elaborately dressed quintet. In comparison to the previous week's young pretenders, Kharanga were at the opposite end of music's dress spectrum. There were no bright orange or lime green jogging suits. Rather, each member of the band looked as though he was perpetuating his very own 1980's rock caricature. The guitar player had obviously been watching several old Aerosmith videos and was sporting a knee length flowing leather jacket in the manner of Joe Perry. The lead singer clearly had his sights set on becoming the Mongolian version of Axle Rose with his hair sprouting out from under a trademark bandana. In true rock-and-roll style he was strutting around the stage in dark, shiny leather - and massively unflattering – pants. It all seemed a bit of a cliche, but from the first note the music was better! Much better!

Despite their appearance Kharanga were nowhere near as bad as we had feared. In-fact, they were pretty damn good. They too were singing in Mongolian, but in pleasant contrast to the last performance, they were playing drums and guitars to make things a whole lot more palatable. The gig had begun in true rock style with some heavy licks backed up by some pounding drums and thumping bass lines. Then, after an hour of power ballads, everyone in the audience needed to regroup. So the band displayed their softer side by sitting down, taking out the acoustic guitars and offering a welcome change of pace.

Thirty minutes of soft numbers ended when the smoke machine clicked in and the electric guitars were strapped back on. The veterans went onto display just how much of an established musical force they were by playing another solid hour of material. The ageing five-piece had been heralded as the godfathers of Mongolian rock having been part of the Ulaan Baatar music scene since the late 1980s. Their 'experience' began to show as they wheeled out their final few numbers with the singer taking prompts from song sheets placed in front of him – he had written the tracks so long ago that he had forgotten the words.

It was difficult to get the full Kharanga experience as the language barrier meant we couldn't totally understand what the band had to say. Despite this, I left the gig relatively impressed with Kharanga. They had certainly undone some of the damage done by Ice-Top. Their performance gained a deservingly positive review where I lauded their music, but made fun of the singer's trousers. I had little idea how much of an institution those pants were in Mongolia and how much of an influence Kharanga would have on my stay in the country.

Meeting Mr Kharanga

About a month after the concert, I and the other i-to-i volunteers were sitting having Chinese food at a little restaurant on a back street between Sukhbaatar Square and the State Department Store. As we tucked into our fried rice and dumplings, I spotted a slightly worse for wear version of the group's lead singer staggering past our table. The figure was totally unmistakable. He was decked out in the exact same getup as at his recent show. I decided that it wasn't everyday you get the chance to rub

111

shoulders with a rock institution, so I ambled over to him and asked if he would mind if I had my picture taken with him. He agreed, and as I stood there with his arm clasped firmly around my shoulder, I began to notice just how monumentally drunk he was and that he was barely able to stand upright.

Once the pictures had been taken, I bade farewell to Mr. Kharanga and retreated to my table feeling very satisfied with the new photo that sat on my roll of film. However, things were not finished as he soon followed me and began to drill us with questions in very slurred Mongolian. As we didn't have a clue what he was saying, we had very few answers. He began to grow increasingly frustrated with our lack of response before he slugged back his vodka, gave a dismissive flail of his arm and strutted away to his own table. His departure was only temporary, however. He quickly returned with a rather bemused looking lady who turned out to be his English-speaking sister who, very politely, asked what the hell was going on. We explained that three of us were journalists who had attended his latest show and had written reviews in our respective newspapers.

With the rock legend seated at our table once more, we chatted via his sister's interpretation and were treated to the story of a life based around rock n roll excess. Not only did he have several ex-wives, one of whom now lived in America with two of his children, but he had also been in jail on more than one occasion for smoking marijuana. This was still a relatively unusual offence in Mongolia – alcohol being the majority of the population's drug of choice. The sister went on to explain that, because of his behaviour, he didn't have too much to do with the running of the band. Whenever they had a gig the guitarist would simply give him a call to wake him from his drug or alcohol induced slumber, so as to direct him to the venue.

Throughout the conversation, the bandanna clad figure drank a succession of large vodkas and began to sway dramatically. His sister obviously figured it was time to get him home, so she called the rest of the family through and ushered them towards the car. However, our new found rock-n-roll buddy was clearly enjoying his international fame and refused to leave until he had introduced his son to us and shared a toast with both him and us. The boy was twelve and didn't seem to appreciate the large wine glass full of vodka! His dad eventually left the restaurant having been almost forcibly pushed out. Before he finally departed, he left us with the only words in English he uttered all evening, the immortal quote: "My job to rock!"

Partying with Kharanga

Having been to the concert and having met the man himself, I was a big Kharanga fan. If there had been a Kharanga fan club, I would have signed up on the spot. Interestingly, even though we were enamoured by Mongolia's rock legends, we didn't actually know the singer's name. We just called him 'Mr Kharanga'. Nonetheless, our two encounters with him had been awesome! To our delight, we would soon discover, our relationship with

Mongolian rock music was far from over and would provide us with some fantastic entertainment.

Our next encounter came three weeks or so later. It was a Friday evening, but we were planning to have a bit of a quiet one as the following day we would be taking a tip to the Terelje National Park and had a very early start. We had a couple of beers at Steppe Inn and then headed to KhanBrau - a German themed bar in central UB - ready to enjoy some German food and a couple more beers.

Those plans came unstuck when, as we ate, we spotted the tell-tale glistening of leather pants. Upon further investigation we discovered they were accompanied by the bandana and sunglasses. Kharanga was in the house! Straight away, we all thought it would be cool to party with the man himself. So, we decided we would risk the prospect of facing the journey to Terelje the following day with a raging hangover. After all, it wasn't every day you got a chance to paint the town red with a rock legend.

To kick things off, we strutted up to Kharanga's table, where the singer was seated with other members of the band, and presented a bottle of vodka. We were welcomed heartily. A full four minutes later the bottle was empty and Mitch and I were being squeezed into Mr Kharanga's Mercedes along with the rest of the band and a couple of assorted hangers on. There were eight of us crammed into the car as we drove out of the city towards some wasteland a few kilometres away where we were safe enough for Mr Kharanga to reveal some of the substances that had got him arrested.

I am not exactly sure how long we were out of the city, but by the time we made our way back to the urban sprawl darkness was starting to descend and we were already a fair way from sobriety. Mr Kharanga then took us back to visit his apartment and custom-made recording studio. It would have been great material for the arts and culture section on page six of the Post but, unfortunately, my journalistic instincts had been dulled by our earlier endeavours and any report I would have managed may well have been severely lacking in detail.

From the studio, we moved downstairs to the basement, where we found a bar and full-size snooker table. The vodka quickly appeared from behind the bar and we were soon smashing the balls around the table – very badly. Our host and his buddies had clearly had lots of practice and managed to sink a succession of reds and colours. Mitch and I, on the other hand, struggled to pot a ball. After three or four frames and several vodkas, we were in a pretty shabby state, so we decided to head for home. We bade the rock legend a fond adieu and headed into the night.

We may have already been feeling the effects of socializing with a rock band, but our problems had only just begun and they started to grow once we tried to find our way home. We had arrived by car and wound our way through row upon row of apartment blocks. This had completely robbed us of our bearings, leaving us ambling around the suburbs with very little clue as to our exact whereabouts.

It took us almost half-an-hour of aimless wandering to categorically confirm that the majority of Ulaan Baatar's apartment blocks looked the same, that we recognized none of our surroundings and we were in fact magnificently lost. As it was late and we were in the middle of a housing estate, there were also no cabs about. It was frighteningly cold and we began to fear spending the night in sub-zero temperatures. I began to envisage my obituary written in my local newspaper: "Froze to death whilst inebriated in a Mongolian house estate". It wasn't a great scenario! Thankfully, after what felt like hours of chaotic drifting around the outskirts of the city we eventually managed to find what looked like a main. A few minutes later, we were able to flag a cab and head home. Crisis averted.

Farewell dance with Kharanga

After our heavy drinking, snooker playing night on the tiles, Kharanga was always going to live in my memory. However, our encounters with the rock god were far from over. Just prior to leaving Mongolia, Mitch, Ryan and I were in one of UB's disco clubs enjoying some good Korean beer and some terrible Mongolian dance music. We were happily dancing away - badly - when we noticed something of a commotion at the far side of the dance floor. At first we paid it no attention, but soon the young Mongolian party-goers began to gravitate towards whatever it was leaving the dance floor looking rather sparse. So, out of sheer curiosity, we followed suit. In the midst of the small crowd that

116

had gathered was a short chubby man in leather pants, wearing sunglasses and a bandana. Kharanga was in the house! again. Just as in our previous meetings, Mr. Kharanga was a long way from sobriety. He greeted us with a manly hug and a lot of incoherent shouting.

After a few obligatory wine glass sized shots of vodka, we all ploughed onto the dancefloor. We genuinely felt like the coolest kids in school next to our famous friend and were quickly strutting our stuff. Kharanga seemed a little less enthused at dancing and simply stood in one place and made a token effort at moving from side to side.

Were I in a slightly more sober state, I would have begun to wonder what a die-hard rock musician was doing in a cheesy club that played nothing but second-rate pop music. However, we had preceded the disco club with a visit to Tse, which ensured I didn't really care what he was doing there. I was just enjoying the party. When the music stopped though, we got a surprise. A hip-hop act sauntered out onto stage and began to sing a number that had dominated Mongolian radio for the past month.

Suddenly, Kharanga seemed to sober up and he stared across at them with a confusing sense of pride written across his face. He then pointed to them and slapped himself on the chest. With a touch of translation from an English speaking passer-by, we found out that the boys on stage were his protégés. The studio we had visited in his house was where he was working as producer for several new Mongolian bands. Again, had I been sober, it would have had the makings of an impressive story.

The rock influence was clear to see in the young men on stage. Where Ice-Top had been dressed in bright tracksuits, these dudes were dressed all in black and gray and looked almost fearsome – one was even offering a nod to the master by wearing a dark bandana and sunglasses. Their song was not too bad either. I understood none of the words, but it had a heavy sound and soaring lyrics. With such an influence over younger Mongolian music Kharanga looked set to be in the house for a few years at least. It is just a shame Ice-Top had not sought his advice.

Postscript: *This chapter may sound little more than a self-indulgent recounting of drunken exploits. In some ways, that might be true. However, a theme that has stuck with me since my time in Mongolia is that as Mongolia is such a small country there were so many opportunities to get into the very heart of the country and do things that in other countries would be impossible: such as party with the country's most famous rock band. The following chapter may also sound rather self-indulgent, but it too follows this theme.*

7. MONGOLIA'S TOP GOALKEEPER

Adjusting to living in Mongolia was never quite plain sailing. As I hope this book has already shown, life there was very different to the UK. But, it was an amazing place, so I settled in relatively comfortably. Obviously, I missed my family and friends and I can't deny that I also began to crave the odd home comfort. However, the absence of various morsels of western food, English cable TV and soft toilet paper were a nuisance, but nothing more. I could certainly live without them. The only major void in my life that was left gaping was the one that in England was ordinarily filled with football. When I left home I exchanged chilly afternoons in Stockport, Grimsby and Oldham for sub-zero ones in UB. In so doing I was wrenched away from my footy.

To compensate for the lack of direct footballing contact, it quickly became routine for Fran and I to brave the winter snows, head for the Internet café and follow the Division 2 promotion race from afar. (Soon after arriving in UB we had discovered that I supported QPR and Fran followed Plymouth Argyle, the two teams at the top of English football's third tier. This gave us plenty to debate in Tse during the cold Mongolian nights). Back in England, my love for QPR had been very intimate. I regularly went to games and followed their fortunes religiously in the British media. However, in Mongolia, this love-affair became something of a long-distance relationship. Our only contact came via the web. With the eight hour time difference, games usually finished around 1 am Mongolian-time, when I was either tucked up in bed or equally cozy in a bar somewhere. To compound my dislocation from the team I loved, the heavy snow, howling winds and bone chilling temperatures made slipping on the boots and going for a sly game in the park almost impossible.

My state of footballing despair lasted for well over a month before a chance encounter in the State Department Store brought a chink of light. It came whilst Fran and I were searching for Mongolian football shirts in the sports department. We were trying – and failing - to explain to the clerk what we were looking for, when a small Brazilian guy stepped in to ask if he could help. We explained that we were looking for football shirts as souvenirs, but were not having much luck. This caused him to burst out laughing, before he explained that football in Mongolia was not quite the same as it was in the west and that Mongolia barely even had a team let alone a shirt that fans could buy.

This little interlude quickly sparked a prolonged conversation about football, which culminated in Jardel inviting us to go play five-a-side with the team he coached. Such an invitation certainly had Fran and I very excited, but we were both quick to check that we would be playing indoors. He reassured us that we would, but made us slightly nervous when he explained that he played with a few of Mongolia's national team. As we wandered off for lunch, Fran and I began to debate whether we had got ourselves in over our head. Would we be able to hold our own with a Brazilian and half of the national team? Thankfully, a touch of journalistic research assuaged my concerns about being embarrassed by a crop of seasoned internationals. Whilst reading an old article on the back page of the Post about the lesser nations in Asian football - of which Mongolia was clearly one - I found a brief history of soccer in the country. It was a surprisingly short read.

They had only ever played one competitive tie, which was contested over two legs in November 2003 against the Maldives - hardly a footballing heavyweight. The first leg was played on frozen Mongolian soil at the Naadam Stadium in UB. The weather conditions were heavily in favor of the home team. The temperature at pitch side dropped as far as twenty-five degrees below zero, a far cry from what the visitors were used to at home. The Maldavian coach was so worried about the effect the cold would have on his players that he refused to bring a full squad to the game. Instead, his team arrived with only fifteen players, meaning that they didn't even have a full quota of substitutes (He clearly didn't want any of his players to pick up a nasty case of frostbite whilst waiting to play). However, despite the sizable advantage that playing at home gave the Mongolians, they failed to make it tell and were beaten 1-0. Unfortunately, that remained the high point of Mongolian football history. In the return leg, the Maldives rattled up an embarrassing twelve unanswered goals.

Despite their international shortcomings, some of the boys were not that bad and we had some feisty games of futsal (a type of five-a-side football designed to focus on close skills). I was delighted that my footballing void was finally being filled. However, things soon moved to a whole new level when Fran and I were selected to play for Jardel's team in a national tournament staged in UB. The competition was being held to celebrate the twenty-third anniversary of the first - and only - Mongolian cosmonaut making his historic journey into space.

Judgerdimidin Gurragcha was a Mongolian air-force mechanic who, in 1981, made the giant leap from runway to launch pad. On March 22, of that year he blasted off from Baikonour in Kazakhstan alongside his Russian colleague V. A. Dzhanibekov on a Soyuz 39 spacecraft. His research mission lasted nearly eight days, the majority of which he spent aboard the Salyut 6 space station. The mission made him a national hero. Only Sukhbaatar and Chinggis Khan now eclipse him in national adoration. The tournament was named Sansar, the 'rough' translation of which is 'universe', in honor of his achievements.

The former cosmonaut's reputation was obviously a big draw as ten teams from locations such as Erdenet in the northwest,

Darkhan and as far afield as Choibalhsan (A mining town in Mongolia's far east which is named after the murderous dictator who, as we discussed earlier, led Mongolia's Stalinist government in the 1950s) made the journey to the Alder Sport Palace in the capital city. Fran and I would play for Jardel's team, UB United.

The palace was a two-tier venue that was built in the Communist days. The term 'palace' was being used pretty liberally as it was rather decrepit. There were a few cool Soviet style murals on the walls, but the brickwork was crumbling and the drains did not smell very nice at all. For a national tournament, it was a pretty small venue. It could house, at most, a few hundred people. It was also not so well-equipped and was in stark contrast to sports facilities in the UK. Upon our arrival, Fran and I blithely asked Jardel where we should go to change. He looked at us with a slightly patronising air of confusion and explained that we should change by the side of the pitch (in full view of all the spectators). We protested that surely there must be somewhere a little more private, but he just laughed and told us we were no longer in England.

Going into the tournament, UB United were apparently amongst the favourites for the competition. Jardel and Co had won it the previous year. However, since then, they had lost a few players to injury and had managed only a disappointing fourth place in a recent competition in Selenge aimag. Jardel believed that the field looked pretty strong as all three of the sides that had finished above United in that tournament were present in UB. The four big fish in the pot were split between the two groups (each group contained five teams). Selenge and ourselves were in Group A, whilst Sansar and Khoromkon (winners in Selenge) were in Group B.

We began our challenge against Erdenet, who were one of the supposedly unfancied sides. I lined up in goal and Fran played in defence. However, despite being heavy favorites, we found it to be anything but a stroll in the park. Erdenet had clearly not read the script and took the lead after only three and a half minutes with a flicked header that nestled in neatly in the bottom corner of my net. Our defensive frailties were plain for all to see and communication was at a premium, with discussion between goalkeeper and defense proving difficult. I was desperately trying to translate my directions from English into my pidgin Mongolian. However, by the time I had got 'cover the right' translated to "baroon" or 'watch out on the left' to "zuun" the attacker was already clear and bearing down on my goal.

We managed to claw our way back into the game with some tough tackling and a sharp finish from our star striker – Mogi. Unfortunately, our parity and confidence were short lived. Erdenet's second goal was very much made in England. Fran and I both lunged at a cross that was played in from the right, only for it to deflect off his shin and rocket into the roof of my net.

UB United went into the half-time interval trailing 2-1 and searching for inspiration. I am not sure where we found it, but we soon managed to claw our way back into the contest with some samba soccer - Mongol style. The yellow shirts of the hometown team were a blur as our passing and incisive running was just too much for the visitors. The 2-1 deficit was soon overturned and transformed into a 4-2 victory. The highlight of the second period was Fran making up for his own goal by jinking past three defenders before drilling it past the keeper. It wasn't the most convincing performance, but we were on track for the next stage of the competition.

Our opening day victory had left us top of group B, justifying our position as one of the pre-tournament favorites. However, in our next contest, we came back down to earth with a bang when we met Selenge. Kick-off was at the ridiculously early time of 9.30 on a Monday morning and the team from the frozen north certainly caught us napping. By 9.35, I had already dug the ball out of the back of my net twice. Some of our defending had left quite a bit to the imagination, but unfortunately so too had some of my goalkeeping. By half time, we were trailing 3-0 and were again looking for an inspirational fight-back. This time we couldn't muster the kind of performance we needed and left the field humbled by the 5-2 score line.

Thankfully, we didn't have to wait long to make amends for our morning mishap. Our next game was against a young side from Sukhbaatar - The most northern town in Mongolia, situated on the Russian border as a transit point on the rail line that runs from Russia to Beijing in China - on the same afternoon (some of the scheduling was far worse than any of our defending). This time, we were awake from the first whistle and threw ourselves into the hectic opening salvos.

By half time, we looked to have bounced back from our morning mishap and had taken a commanding 2-0 lead. The second period was less convincing as our opponents realized that if the scores stayed the same they would be on the train out of Ulaan Baatar. It was backs to the wall stuff for most of the half as they threw everything at us. Only a combination of last-ditch defending, manic goalkeeping and quite often pure luck kept us alive and still vying for the final place in the semi-finals. The hard-fought result set up a do-or-die affair against Darkhan. The winners would go through; the losers would go home. If it was a draw, neither could be sure of progressing.

Unsurprisingly things were cagey from the outset. Neither side wanted to give anything away as both teams knew what defeat would mean. The first half was a pretty dour affair dominated by cautious, defensive football. It wasn't until the second period, when the pressure began to tell, that the game opened up. With only seven minutes left both sides began to realize that although they couldn't afford to lose, a draw may not have been good enough either. The boys from Darkhan began to push forward more and more, paying less attention to defence. This worked out well for us as they left themselves vulnerable at the back to the classic counter attack. Mogi was again auditioning for the role of hero as he raced away and powered one into the bottom corner sending the entire team into some slightly manic celebrations. We even got some backing from the crowd - which had risen to a couple of hundred people - who appeared to be warming to the local boys.

Things were beginning to get exciting as we entered the business end of proceedings. A little spice was added to events as all four of the teams from Selenge had made the semi-finals. The top of group A was set to face the second placed team in Group B and vice versa. Therefore, we were expecting a tough outing against Khoromkhon, who were hot-favourites in Group B. We would have to wait to face those boys however, as Sansar sprang an upset by beating them comfortably in the final group game. This set up a Sansar versus UB United clash in the first semi-final.

Roughly twenty-five seconds into the game and we had quickly realized why Sansar had the beating of Khoromkhon. Some neat passing culminated in their striker sending a pile driver into the bottom corner from about thirteen yards out, leaving me laying flat on the floor wondering what had hit us. The one saving grace was that we had been in this position before. Unfortunately, that gave us scant consolation when, after four minutes, it was two. Our opponents produced some slick passing and movement down our right hand side that was capped by a vicious cross to the far post, where an unmarked attacker nodded it past my despairing dive.

The crowd had gone quiet and our heads had dropped. It was surely time for a comeback akin to our opening game. For a few brief seconds, that appeared to be on the cards when we clawed our way back into the game with a scrappy goal from Mogi. Alas, this appeared to be a false down as we hit the self-destruct button. Twice within the space of a minute I had dug the ball out of my net. On both occasions they were own goals and on both occasions the scorer was my fellow Englishman. 4-1 down and heading out of the competition … it seemed.

Half-time was a pretty somber affair. Jardel tried his utmost to lift our spirits, but things were not looking good. When the second half got underway, Sansar already seemed to be planning for the final as they passed the ball around gently, content to eat up time. For the first five minutes, this plan suited them well and the game dropped into a rut. That was until, Mogi again popped up out of the blue to add another goal to his already impressive tally for the competition. Almost straight away, this began to conjure up images of our previous fight-back and revitalized the entire side.

We threw everything at the opposition who were taken aback by our sudden burst of aggression. The pressure was intense. We crashed the ball off a post and went close on a number of occasions. Sansar were defending so deep that my duties involved simply hurling the ball back towards the other half of the pitch whenever they managed a clearance. Yet, for all our efforts and second half dominance, it looked like the breakthrough would just never come. Then, with less than three minutes on the clock as we laid siege to their goal, the ball ricocheted between three or four players in and around the Sansar goalmouth before somehow nestling in the back of the net – cue chaos and wild celebrations.

All our players and the growing crowd were delirious. But, we still remained one behind and had to get on with it. The clock was counting down as we continued to lay siege to their goal. Yet, as we approached injury time, it looked like we had left it just that little bit too late and would be ruing our poor defending and missed chances.

We knew there could not be too long left when Fran went out left to take a corner. At this stage of the game delivery had to be perfect, but as soon as it left his boot it looked too close to the goalie. It looked like we had wasted our last chance. The keeper dove forward to grasp the ball gratefully to his chest for what should have been a routine take. However, he managed to make a massive miscalculation allowing the ball to squirm through his hands and into the goal – cue even more chaos and even wilder celebrations.

There wasn't even time for the restart as the final whistle blew almost instantly. Our entire squad, including the coach, was celebrating in one massive sprawl in the middle of the park. The Sansar boys looked downcast, dejected and disbelieving. The game had finished 4-4, which meant sudden death extra time. The momentum in the contest was clearly heading in only one direction. Try as they might Sansar could not raise themselves back to their earlier levels. It took less than three minutes for the hitherto quiet Telmen (Our slightly built defender) to put away the goal that gave us victory, his first in the entire competition. The celebrations were wild and our hero was clearly unsure of what to do. He opted for removing his shirt, but, unfortunately, fell over as he dragged it over his head to add a slightly comic ending to our Hollywood style comeback.

We sat back down on the bench thoroughly exhausted, but totally elated. We were in the final, but who would we face? Neither of the options were particularly enticing. Selenge had mauled us to the point of embarrassment in the first round and Khoromkhon were the competition favorites. Their semi produced nowhere near the level of excitement or goals, but it did exhibit a great deal more defensive acumen. Selenge went ahead in the first half, but Khoromkhon's Zulaa was proving to be quite a threat. The 6"4' striker was posing problems both on the floor and in the air. The opinion around the Alder Sport palace was that when Mongoli played its next international game, he should be the team's number one striker. It was no surprise when the big man equalized shortly after the half time interval and from then on Selenge were never really in the game with Zulaa adding the winner for good measure.

The final was to be played the same evening under the added pressure of the UB TV cameras (This was the state run TV channel that broadcasts across the country). They would be showing highlights on the national news that night. I will have to admit to having been a little bit nervous at being on national TV. Although the following comparison doesn't hold too much water as Mongolia is a far smaller country than the UK and the standard of football is soooooo much lower than in England, it was their equivalent of getting coverage on the six o'clock news on the BBC. Even though Mongolia is a small country, plenty of people would be watching me. That had never really been the case when I had played Sunday morning football or Tuesday night 5-a-side in England.

The final had a massive sense of déjà vu as we conceded the first goal yet again. However, after all the drama of the previous rounds, this barely fazed us. We had come back from the same position on two occasions already and were well prepared to do it a third time. The scores were level again after five minutes when Telmen repeated his semi-final heroics by stabbing one in at the far post - fortunately this time, though, his shirt stayed firmly on his back. It was all looking good as we battled hard against a far more physical side. Zulaa was causing trouble but nothing that had me unduly worried. Parity at half time seemed within touching distance, but, yet again, events took a familiar twist. Some slack marking allowed Khoromkhon to get three men forward with Zulaa rounding off a slick move with a cool finish. The TV audience would have been unimpressed at our defending. We trudged in at half time knowing we simply had to repeat the heroics of our semi-final that morning.

The chances of such events looked remote as Khoromkhon came out bristling with steely resolve. They had clearly seen the other teams come unstuck against our second-half rallies and were keen not to befall the same fate. Things were cagey as they looked to defend their lead and we daren't get too adventurous in case

Zulaa were to punish us on the break. It took seven minutes of the half for the breakthrough to come. Unfortunately, when it did, it came at the wrong end. Until that point, we had kept their powerful center forward under wraps in the second period, but one slight mistake at the back and he slipped his man to get clear on goal. He kept his composure well to deposit the ball past my left hand and into the far bottom corner ending the game as a contest ... apparently.

What followed the third Khoromkhon goal definitely gave the TV cameras something to shoot. The two-goal deficit seemed to wake us up and UB United launched yet another slightly implausible comeback. We had come to the conclusion that a deft passing game was having no effect against our heavyweight opponents. So, we opted for the long ball game. This involved me heaving the ball from my penalty area into the opposition's box and hoping we could get a head on it. The tactic looked as though it would pay dividends, as Munkhbadral, Khoromkhon's goalkeeper and captain, appeared to be uncertain in the air. Their defenses finally gave way under our bombardment when he came a long way to punch and failed to get there. No one could tell whether the ball touched his fingertips or Fran's head, but it sailed in – cue chaos once more. We then had about five minutes to complete our salvage operation. This time, though, we only needed three.

For the entire competition our winger Saruula had been flaying his shots high, wide and handsome. On occasion he had even managed to reach the upper deck of seating with a couple of seriously speculative efforts. However, he picked an opportune moment to hit the target for the first time. I was among the many who winced as he prepared to strike a cross-field pass that had been knocked his way, but then, to the amazement of me, the entire crowd and probably also himself, he smashed a thunderbolt of a shot that took slight deflection past the keeper and in. We had done it again – cue unprecedented chaos and unrestrained celebrations.

Whereas in the semi the whistle followed straight after our equalizer, this time we had two minutes still to play and, unfortunately, the drama was not over. Khoromkhon kicked off in search of the lead they had let slip. With only seconds on the watch, an innocuous challenge from one of our players was penalized by the referee. To the entire sport palace's collective amazement a penalty was given - it looked to be neither a foul nor to be in our penalty area.

Our entire team looked distraught. It is safe to assume our protestations were both vocal and impassioned. Had the referee understood some of my colourful British language, I may well have found myself on the receiving end of a yellow or red card. However, we made no headway and it looked like everything was going wrong at the very death. With the cameras focused on my goal one of the opposition's midfielders stepped up to the spot. There is no knowing what went through his mind as he ran up, but without doubt, the pressure told and the ball ballooned spectacularly over the crossbar to safety. The relief was palpable.

We had survived to play our second golden goal of the day.

Our second game of sudden death did not have the happy ending we thought we were destined for. It took less than a minute for the second penalty of the evening to be awarded to Khoromkhon. For a second time, there were impassioned protestations, but to our disappointment this time there would be no mistake. Zulaa stepped up and despite me getting across and getting fingers to the ball he smashed it into the bottom corner to end the tournament. The Khoromkhon players began a string of celebrations that mirrored our own earlier in the day, whilst we sat there dejected. It took Mogi to haul me from the ground. The disappointment was such that I just couldn't muster the energy to stand. As he did so the UB TV cameras panned from Khoromkhon to us. It was a sorry looking shot.

The post-tournament presentations were a lengthy process as Gurragcha himself distributed prizes to all the different age groups who had competed (There had also been a juniors and over 50s competition). The cosmonaut then got on to the individual honors with prizes for the top goal-scorer, the best defender and the tournament's best keeper. Zulaa had edged out Mogi as the top marksman and one of Sansar's defenders took home his respective prize. The Defense Minister then made another long and official sounding announcement, but instead of someone going up to collect a prize, nothing happened. There was an eerie and quite uncomfortable silence. Half a minute or so later, people began turning round and looking at me. Saruula then slapped me on the back and told me to go up – I had won. Somehow I was the goalkeeper of the tournament.

Mr. Gurragcha was dressed in a military uniform with an unsurprisingly large array of medals. He was very polite, but unfortunately spoke no English. So, I shook his hand, took my trophy and said *bayarlala*, at which he smiled warmly. There were many people in Mongolia I would have liked to have shared a few words with, but couldn't. Gurragcha was very much at the top of this list – a real life astronaut and national hero.

Ever since the presentation, I have wondered whether I won the award on merit or got it out of a sense of novelty value. In truth, some of the competition was not the strongest. Even though Khoromkhon came out on top, Munkhbadral in their goal had failed to impress and his mistake in the final could even have cost them the tournament. Similarly, in the semi-final, Sansar were ahead with only seconds left when their keeper dropped the ball into his own goal. Maybe my lack of overt mistakes and the two clean sheets in the group-stage were enough to sway the judges. I will never know.

As well as I think I played and as much as I believe in myself and my own ability, I have to acknowledge that I was by far the least conspicuous player in the entire tournament. Even before a ball was kicked I was getting a lot of attention. UB United lined up in tasteful yellow shirts. I, on the other hand, was provided with a fluorescent orange and green goalkeeper's jersey. Coupled with my shaven head and six-foot frame this made me stand out like some form of footballing beacon. Once the games began, my on-the-field demeanour did little to help me blend in. The majority of the home-grown goalkeepers were quiet, content to allow their coaches and defenders to bark instructions around the pitch. I was far less restrained and continuously screamed instructions at those in my defensive line whenever the ball even showed a hint of appearing in our half – in true English style.

There was little chance of me going anywhere on the night after the tournament. I was staying firmly at Chez Batmunkh to watch TV and try to catch a glimpse of myself. I soon found out that we did indeed make national news. UB TV showed pictures of Mr. Gurragcha and then cut to footage of Zulaa running up and smashing the penalty home. The camera then zoomed in on me punching the floor in frustration and mouthing a few choice words in disappointment. It was a pleasant surprise to make national television, but it was no surprise to anyone when a full-length report appeared on the back-page of the UB Post.

8. ALL MONGOLIANS LOVE JOHNNY CASH

By mid-March the weather in northeast central Asia was beginning to abate. Sadly, it was not relenting all that much. Temperatures of 30 degrees below zero had given way to an average of ten below. This meant that there was still plenty of snow and ice lurking on the potholed streets of Ulaan Baatar. The heavy cold and even heavier pollution was beginning to get just a little bit depressing. Even though we were making every effort to enjoy everything the city had to offer, I was beginning to tire of spending my weekends within its smoky confines.

The only place outside of the capital that we had visited was Darkhan and our wolf hunting expedition was beginning to feel like a distant memory. However, as our first trip had taught us, finding a worthwhile and accessible destination was not going to be easy. Regardless of the fact that spring was coming along fast, it remained way too cold to consider some of the more remote areas of the country. Places like the epically proportioned Lake Khovsgol would remain frozen until at least May. Even closer options such as the Terelje national park, which was a mere 80 kilometres from UB, were still snowbound. The elemental restrictions left only one serious alternative in our quest to escape the city: the Gobi.

I was excited about visiting the Gobi as it genuinely sparked my sense of adventure. It was a place that conjured images of exploits that came straight out of the pages of comic books. It was also home to a huge array of dinosaurs. Or, at least it had been. During the first half of the twentieth century, many explorers such as the famed American Roy Chapman Andrews (Who was, apparently, the inspiration for Indiana Jones) plundered the sands of the Gobi unearthing scores of fossils and skeletons that now sit in museums across the western world. In the second half of the twentieth century, they were followed by their Soviet equivalents who took the majority of the remaining natural treasures north to Russia. However, a few traces were still on show at the Natural History Museum in UB. So, in preparation for our own desert expedition we decided to pay it a visit.

We found that whilst it was a tremendously interesting institution it had, like most of Mongolia, been starved of funds and was beginning to show signs of decay with some of the windows being cracked and some of the plaster peeling from the walls. Regardless of the poor maintenance though, the dinosaur section boasted some impressive displays. In terms of both sheer scale and ferocity, the star attraction was without doubt a full size Tyrannosaurus. The Tyrannosaurus Baatar was a species of the infamous carnivore that roamed the areas that now make up present day Mongolia. A mature adult could reach up to 40 feet in length, 15 to 20 feet in height and between five and seven tons in weight. The one that was now permanently resident in UB took up two floors of the museum and dwarfed everything else in the building.

There were also some other interesting pieces too. For example, there was a full-size velociraptor - like the evil ones in Jurassic Park - that somehow managed to still look unbelievably scary despite having been dead for millions of years. There was also a display known as the 'Fighting Dinosaurs', which featured the skeletons of two dinosaurs that had been buried during a sandstorm whilst the two creatures had been locked in combat.

Trans-Mongolian

The dinosaur attractions notwithstanding, reaching the most areas of the Gobi was not going to be feasible. First of all, none of us were too keen on the prospect of taking a 24-hour Jeep ride across harsh, frozen, snow covered terrain. That would certainly be a frightfully uncomfortable trip. This was the only way to get to the majority of towns and camping grounds. Secondly, we had to be back in the office on Monday morning - lord knows what stories of corruption and political inefficiency would be sat on our desks when we got back. Fortunately, there was a relatively easy option. The town of Sainshand could be reached without too much difficulty and in relative comfort, since it was situated on the main railway line, 150 miles north of the Chinese border.

The Mongolian national railway cuts the country in half from the Russian border in the north to the Chinese frontier in the south. It is part of the epic Trans-Mongolian railway that runs all the way from Moscow to Beijing via Ulaan Baatar. Thankfully, our trip would not be on such a grand scale. Sainshand - the only 'major' city in the Gobi region - was only 450 km from UB, meaning that instead of the week it would have taken to complete the whole journey from Europe to Asia, we would be travelling for a trifling nine hours each way.

There are two classes of travel on the domestic rail services that operate along the Trans Mongolian route: hard and soft. The hard seats were just as they sounded, amounting to little more than metal bunks fastened to the wall in an open carriage. The soft seats, on the other hand, were far more luxurious. They came four to a cabin and had the added comfort of a mattress, albeit a very firm and narrow one. We decided it would be provident to purchase our tickets in advance so as to ensure we got the highest standard of travel. The mood within the group was that a nine-hour journey across the steppe and through the desert was no time to be experimenting with a carriage full of sweaty herdsmen.

Purchasing our tickets proved to be no easy feat. The entire staff of the Trans Mongolian Railways office in Ulaan Baatar had a combined English vocabulary of approximately nine words, which roughly matched that of our Mongolian. Communication quickly degenerated into a combination of pointing at the phrasebook and some improvised sign language. The process seemed to take forever. There was a great deal of confusion on both sides. The staff didn't really get that we wanted soft tickets and we weren't sure what the staff were trying to communicate to us. There was plenty of back and forth but progress was slow. However, after almost an hour of discussions and gesticulations we were given a handful of white slips of paper printed with Cyrillic script and a picture of a train – success, we presumed. By this point in my stay, I had succeeded in reading Cyrillic script and was pretty sure the tickets said Sainshand.

There were seven of us heading for the desert. Three other volunteers from the same I-to-I program - Martha, Loti and Rog - joined Mitch, Fran, Ryan and I. Martha and Loti were taking a gap year before going to university and had come to Mongolia to work at the Mongolian Youth Development Centre's institution for girls involved in or at risk from prostitution. Rog was in his thirties and teaching English at a local catering college. We were set to meet at 9.15 am, thirty minutes before our train was due to leave. However, thanks to a rather vigorous night in Steppe Inn, Tse and somewhere else I don't quite recall, I arrived nursing a slightly pained head and queasy stomach only four minutes before we were scheduled to leave.

Our compartment, although basic, was comfortable. There were four bunks complete with bedding, a table and two sporadically functioning lights. As comfy as we quickly made ourselves, we soon faced a major ventilation problem. Mitch, Ryan and I were sharing one compartment and since all three of us had been burning the midnight oil in downtown UB the previous evening, it quickly began to take on the aroma of a Mongolian brewery. In winter, the trains are heated and in summer they are air-conditioned. Because of this, the windows are fastened firmly closed. With nowhere for the unpleasant, hung-over aroma to go, the cabin soon began to mirror UB and fill up with some overtly noxious fumes.

At just before ten, we eased away from the platform and headed off slowly in the direction of China. As we inched our way south, the scenery on view through our permanently closed window went through some dramatic changes. After we left the city, we moved out onto the steppe, which was just beginning to thaw, but, like the city, still exhibited an ample covering of snow. However, in refreshing contrast to the urban version, the rural snowfall was white, crisp and untainted by pollution. The changes over the course of the journey were quite stark, but since we were covering such a large distance they took place gradually and we barely noticed the snow giving way to sprawling grassland, which then in turn receded into the sands of the northern Gobi.

Once we had drawn clear of Ulaan Baatar, population density also decreased dramatically and settlements became sparser and sparser. In the grassland areas, we spotted the occasional ger with isolated herdsmen tending their animals. Then, once we made it into the desert, we would notice isolated settlements that peaked through the sand before disappearing once more as we pulled out of view.

The only major town along our route was a wind-swept place named Choir. It was a grim looking locale that in its Communist heyday was home to Mongolia's largest Soviet air base. In the 1960s, Moscow had supplied Mongolia with a small quantity of MiG fighter jets that were based in Choir. However, since 1990 the Mongolians have lacked the technology and facilities to maintain and fly them. They have instead, like the dinosaurs that inhabited the region before them, become fossils of an era long gone. Consequently, all we really saw in Choir were some shabby looking apartment buildings - even shabbier than in UB - and the shell of the old air base.

Arriving in the Gobi

We drew into Sainshand at approximately 7.00pm on a balmy desert evening. As soon as we stepped onto the platform, the first thing to strike us was the earliest beginnings of a spectacular sunset. The blue sky was beginning to lose its crisp brightness and a combination of oranges and purples was just starting to drift across the horizon. Shortly after, we were also struck by the fact that it was rather warm.

Having come from icy streets and biting winds, a balmy desert evening was a very welcome change. We had jumped off the train wearing our padded winter clothing, but soon found ourselves quickly shedding layers. As beautiful as the sunset and weather were, though, we didn't have too much time to admire them. We had some practical issues to deal with first: We needed tickets for our return to the capital the next day.

Sainshand station's ticket office amounted to little more than a frosted window in the waiting room wall, which measured barely one foot by two feet. Upon our arrival, it was closed but I could see and hear activity from behind the glass. I knocked three times and waited … and waited. No-one answered. It wasn't until a crowd of thirty or forty people had built up that the lady behind the counter saw fit to open her window. It seemed that even though we were firmly in the post-Communist era, old habits clearly die hard and western-style customer service was not a major concern for Mongolia's railway staff.

I managed to fight off the throng of del-covered arms to get in first and ask for seven tickets to Ulaan Baatar the next day. She looked at me with a combination of disdain and confusion, shook her head and began serving a toothless old lady who had snuck under my left armpit to get to the counter. I continued to wait, showing a bit of western naivety, hoping that the ticket lady would return to me after she had served the old woman.

Unfortunately, I had no such luck and after a couple more people were served whilst I stood there with no clue as to what was going on, I decided it was time to interject. I managed to elbow a scruffy looking herdsman out of the way and yelled at the ticket lady in my best Mongolian, "*ugui Bi*" (No me!). She stood there, stared at

144

me, rolled her eyes, wrote '1900' on a piece of paper and motioned for me to leave. So, with my tail firmly between my legs, I rejoined the group and confessed that I had no tickets and very little idea how to get them. We were at a loss as to what 1900 meant. We guessed it was either a time reference or a train number, but really could not be sure which.

The actual town of Sainshand is just over two kilometres from the railway station. So, we decided to head out on foot whilst the sun was not completely set and the light was still good. There was the pleasant surprise of a paved road leading all the way into the centre of town, but we took a detour via the town's Tank Monument which sat atop some imposing sand dunes that overlooked the town.

It was a memorial to Mongolia's fighting men and was along the same lines as the imposing national Zaisan Memorial that sits on top of a hill 5km outside UB. However, whereas Zaisan was still well-kept and regularly maintained, this version was -like the fighter planes to the north - decaying with little hope of resurrection. The tank was painted a dark olive green colour, which seemed rather strange as we were in the desert, but was covered in graffiti and was missing the roof to its turret. Despite the damage and a vast array of broken and emptied vodka bottles that were strewn around, it provided an imposing silhouette as the last embers of the desert sun disappeared below the western horizon.

Once it had gone almost completely dark, we decided to use the light from the town below to help navigate our way down the dunes and find a hotel. As we were in a remote corner of the country, we were a little sheepish about finding anywhere to stay at all, let alone anywhere decent. We were so worried in fact that we had even considered the possibility of sleeping in the sand under the stars. However, finding accommodation proved to be an oddly simple process. As we reached the bottom of the dunes and rejoined the paved road, we could clearly see a modern square block of a building that was well lit, painted a crisp white and exhibited a large neon sign that said 'hotel'.

Mongolia is not Switzerland and some of its accomodation are not what one might describe as lavish. Even the UlaanBaatar Hotel in the capital had not been refurbished since the collapse of Communism. However, once inside Sainshand's best hotel, we were very pleasantly surprised. The lobby was clean, freshly decorated and air–conditioned. There was even satellite TV playing in the corner. Things got even better when we were shown to our rooms and found modern, clean bathrooms. In comparison to what I used at the Batmunkhs, where the bathroom and toilet were cramped and dated, it was paradise.

After a night in some smoky bars the previous evening, a nine-hour train ride and a two-kilometre hike into a town, a shower was very much the order of the day. So, I grabbed one of the nice white towels that came with the room and headed into the bathroom in anticipation of getting nice and clean. However, alas, it was at this point that reality began to strike. I opened the faucet

146

in expectation of a surging current of clean warm water. Instead, a dribble of something sludgy and brown greeted me.

Having been unable to get a shower, we at least hoped we could console ourselves with a good meal. All we had eaten on the train were Pringles, a few pastries and instant noodles. So, I was absolutely ravenous. Our hopes were heightened when we found a well-decorated restaurant on the ground floor with a menu full of hearty local grub. Mongolian food may not be the most wide-ranging or flavourful, but it is filling.

Unfortunately, we were in for our second successive dose of harsh reality in quick succession. As we waited for the waitress, we all made varied choices from the menu. My mouth was watering at the prospect of some *khorshoo* (mutton filled pancakes) and maybe a bowl of noodle soup to go with them. It was only after we had scanned all seven pages of the menu and called her over that she informed us that the only thing on the menu that was actually available was Tsuiven. To compound things, it was nowhere near as good as Azzah's at home!

Disco in the desert

After our disappointing meal, we sat in the restaurant at something of a loose end. Everyone we had spoken too had told us that whilst the Gobi boasted awesome scenery, it was not home to a particularly lively social scene. However, during a lull in our conversation we began to hear the faint tell-tale pounding of dance music. We asked the waitress where we might find some entertainment for the evening and she pointed to a sign for the 'Piramid' disco club in the hotel's basement. With few other options, we decided it would have been rude not to sample the delights on offer. So, we headed downstairs to experience the hottest nightspot in the northern Gobi.

Sainshand can only muster a population of around 20,000 people. However, it appeared that the majority of its inhabitants who were below the age of 19 had turned out for the evening. They had found quite the establishment to frequent. The whole place was darkened. What little light there was reflected around the dance-floor by a massive disco ball. The walls were painted black and were covered in fluorescent Egyptian themed paintings that suggested the spelling of Piramid was something of a mistake. Regardless of the somewhat questionable décor and quite appalling techno music that was being played, Piramid proved to be one of my favourite nights in Mongolia.

We sat down on three couches positioned at the side of the dance floor to enjoy a couple of beers and watch the local teenagers bust some of their best dance moves. The kids weren't bad, but the music they were dancing too was just awful - worse than Ice Top - and none of us were sure how much more we could take. It was as the DJ played yet another interminably dull number that I came up with a plan. I had my discman in the pocket of my coat and inside I had a CD that would be a complete change of pace: Johnny Cash. So, I fished it out and sidled my way over to the DJ's booth, handed him the CD and held up two fingers in the hope that he would play track two for us. Once he had taken it, I returned to my seat and we waited.

Nearly ten minutes and three more terrible songs later we were still waiting and I was beginning to give up hope. It was just then that we heard the first licks of acoustic guitar burst through as the final bars of the previous song faded away. The teenagers on the dancefloor stopped in their tracks with looks of complete confusion written across their face. How could they dance to this? After less than one verse of *Sea of Heartbreak* (On the American Recordings), they all slowly moved back to their seats leaving the dance floor empty and everyone in the club confused.

At that point, it didn't look like my idea was going too well and my wild assertions that all Mongolians loved Johnny Cash were looking unfounded. Then, all of a sudden, as the Man in Black strummed his way into the chorus, a couple of tables near the back of the club began to whoop and clap in time. Instantly, we all joined in and soon others around the club were following suit. It was almost like being in a redneck bar in deepest Tennessee! At one point, we looked across the room to see a table of young men with wide grins across their faces happily playing air guitar with all their heart. The atmosphere had changed so much that at the height of the number I seriously had to restrain myself from letting out a massive yee-haw.

When the final few bars of the song faded away the ambiance soon descended back into the subdued. The DJ went back to his collection of sub-standard pop-music, the guys put down their air guitars, the teenagers got back on the dance floor and I went and recovered my CD. Even though the reversion had been quick and total, our brief little interlude had been a classic. We left not too long after assuming, quite rightly, that nothing could top hearing Johnny Cash in a misspelled Egyptian themed disco club in a remote corner of southern Mongolia.

Into the Gobi

After taking breakfast in the hotel – Tsuiven again – we decided that there was nothing else for it but to get to grips with the desert first hand. Lonely Planet suggested a gentle hike to an outcrop of dark volcanic rocks two or three hours out of town. On what was a very bright day, these were clearly visible and looked well within striking distance. After stocking up on as much water as we could easily carry, we headed through the dusty outskirts of the town on the first tentative steps of what would become an epic hike.

The railway line that had carried us the previous day signified the border between the town and the wasteland beyond. Prior to reaching it we passed heaps of scrap metal, dilapidated apartment blocks and piles of decaying garbage. However, once we crossed the tracks, it all dissipated and gave way to endless sand and windswept gers. For the first few hundred meters a paved road aided us, but this soon petered out and we were getting sand in our boots.

Even though we had left the confines of Sainshand, we were still in Mongolia and, consequently, were not totally exempt from the outbreaks of uncontrolled garbage and pollution that plague the country. Therefore, it was no surprise when we began to find our path out into the heart of the desert increasingly cluttered. But, in contrast to UB, this was not the usual array of soda cans and noodle wrappers.

Just as with Choir to the north, it was clear that the Soviets had had a military presence in Sainshand. We were not too far from the Chinese border, so we presumed that the town was once quite strategic for the Soviets. As we trudged past an array of demolished buildings, we began to notice several objects poking through the sand. The first thing to catch my eye was a heavily rusted metal cylinder, which on closer inspection quite alarmingly turned out to be a mortar shell!

Upon glancing around a little further, we noticed there were several more with their heads jutting just above the ground. Doing a little quick maths told us that they were at least fourteen years old, but a glance at the rust levels suggested they had been there since well before Mongolia was left to clean up its own desert. Their age led us to believe that they would not be live and were unlikely to remove any of our limbs. However, at no point were we completely sure. If we had been mistaken and were caused serious injury the chances of getting the fast efficient care we would require were minimal. The nearest decent hospital was over a thousand miles away – in another country.

The mortars were not alone, though. We found cups, bags and

even rubber boots peaking through the snow. The whole place had a very strange feeling. It was as though we were walking through a strange combination of cemetery and museum. The ideology and government that had put those things in Mongolia was confined to the annals of history, yet the minutiae that had sustained it still sat in the sand before us.

Once we had passed the relics, we continued on what was quickly becoming a quest to find a corner of the vast and remote land that was genuinely unspoiled. As we continued to trudge away from the town, the desert began to open out. It seemed that no matter how hard we walked the rocks were perpetually teetering on the horizon. The afternoon soon started to get hotter and hotter, our walking pace began to drop and the distance between our destination and ourselves appeared to be growing.

It took almost three hours for us to reach the first few darkened stones at the base of the rocks. By the time we arrived, we were exhausted and were in desperate need of a sit-down and long drink of water. From our position at the base of the rocks, we looked up into the hills and decided to pick a point to head for. They seemed to sprawl for miles, so we decided on a peak that was both pretty high and pretty close.

The climb to the top was difficult. Unlike the sands we had just crossed, the rocks were uneven and unstable causing the occasional slip and making progress even slower than before. However, once at the top, we found a panoramic view like none I had ever witnessed. The golden dunes below were uninhibited and disappeared over countless horizons whilst the sun shone down from the clear blue sky. After over three hours hiking, Sainshand was barely visible in the distance. We basked in the sense of achievement, but were rather alarmed at how far we were from the train that was due to take us home.

Suffering in the heat

If we had thought reaching the rocks was hard work, we had no idea how badly the elements would begin to take their toll on the return leg. The first problem that began to affect us was fatigue. Hiking through the sand had seriously taken it out of our calf muscles. As this started to have an impact, we soon found that the group was beginning to stretch out over about a mile of desert like a thin line of black dots against the golden backdrop.

Those of us at the front of the death march ploughed on looking for some semblance of shade, whilst those at the back chose to battle the heat with a slower, more sedate pace. Dehydration was also becoming a major factor as the day wore on. We had only brought as much water as we could carry and consequently had to balance thirst against the reservation of our supply.

It wasn't until later in the day that we began to notice other symptoms of facing the harsh desert elements. Having come from the snows of Ulaan Baatar, we were not really prepared for the twenty-five degree heat and blazing sun. This, coupled with the slight breeze that worked to mask just how strong the sun's rays actually were, ensured some dramatic changes in skin coloration.

As our group was primarily English and Canadian, there was a general trend of going from pale to pink and then in some cases onto an almost purple colour.

The worst victim of sunburn was myself. Without really noticing, the sun had scorched the outline of my t-shirt onto my skin, leaving my forearms, neck and throat verging on a burgundy colour, whilst my upper arms and torso remained pasty white. However, this was far from my worst problem. The heat had left me sweating profusely, so to temporarily cool myself down I had removed my hat. With no hair to shield my scalp from the rays that were pouring down from above, my head quickly went a deep and particularly frightening colour. The only break was a bleached white line where my sunglasses had been perched on my nose.

I may have exhibited the worst sunburn in the group, but I was by no means the only one suffering. A combination of sun, heat and thirst had sent Martha's face almost the same colour as her violet t-shirt. Mitch had been clever enough to wear his hat for almost the entirety of the walk, this was clearly evident when he removed it and revealed an emphatic line across the top of his forehead: above it was white, below pink.

Perhaps the member of the group who suffered most, though, was our elder statesman, Rog. He made the trip south complete with a heavy padded jacket that had been serving him well on the chilly streets of the capital. However, in the desert, it was proving a massive burden. He already had a large rucksack with supplies and water to carry, making it far easier to wear the jacket than lug it around. Alas, when he did so he began to get alarmingly hot. By the time the streets of Sainshand were fully in view again, he was starting to lag behind and looked in danger of collapse. However, despite the heavy going, Rog and the rest of us made it back into Sainshand ready to get our train. The only problem then was that we had to buy our tickets.

Heading home

The ticket office opened at precisely 7 pm and in the process solved the mystery of what 1900 meant. We purchased our soft seat tickets and waited for the train to arrive at just before eight. My limbs were aching tremendously and I was in desperate need of rest. Unfortunately, the waiting room was crowded and void of empty seats. My only option was to lie down on the cold, hard stone of the platform. This did nothing for my aching muscles, but worked wonders in relieving some of the irritation from my sunburn.

When we finally boarded the train, we discovered that this time we would be forced to share our compartment with a fourth person, a Mongolian heading up to the capital city. Fortunately for him, the odour of stale sweat that we were giving off, was masked by the variety of creams and potions that we were administering to ourselves to alleviate the pains the hike had caused.

9. AT HOME ON THE RANGE

Regardless of the sunburn and blisters that the desert had inflicted upon us, our trip to the Gobi had certainly galvanized our desire to explore the Mongolian countryside further. With the weather getting warmer by the day, Ulaan Baatar quickly became far less restricting and ceased to be the prison it once was. So, with the smell of freedom drifting through our nostrils, we began planning another expedition beyond the city limits. We had in mind the Terelje National Park some eighty kilometres outside UB, which was well known for its rolling hills and the opportunities it offered for both hiking and horse trekking.

We figured the park would provide us with the perfect chance to experience the more traditional side of Mongolian life. Ulaan Baatar is now the capital city and central hub of the country. However, that was not always the case and centralization is, in fact, a relatively recent phenomenon. Until well into the last century, the capital remained extremely small and almost the entire population lived out on the steppe in their gers, maintaining a nomadic lifestyle. Even though we were far from nomads,

Terelje would allow us to spend a night in a ger and to see the type of countryside the Mongols had roamed for generations.

The entire group of I-to-I volunteers – ten of us in all – decided to make the journey, so we hired a minivan to ferry us along the road from the city. To get as much as possible from our weekend, we decided to start bright and early at just after eight on Saturday morning. However, things failed to get off to the brisk start we were hoping for, thanks to the after effects of the previous evening. Mitch and I had been out socializing with Kharanga and were consequently not in the best of health. I managed to pull off a very passable impression of a Mongolian alcoholic lying inert on the sidewalk with my hat wedged over my face whilst Mitch stumbled off in search of bottled water as we waited for the mini-van to show-up. After twenty minutes lapsing in and out of consciousness, the minivan with the rest of the group finally arrived and I was forced to rouse myself from my slumber.

We squeezed ourselves and ten backpacks into the vehicle before pulling away slowly with the rear axle in danger of buckling under the combined weight. Thankfully, there was a thin paved road stretching all the way from UB to deep inside the heart of the park. This little luxury had raised my hopes of managing to catch a few minutes of much needed shut-eye en-route. Alas, I would be disappointed as, although the road was paved, it was far from smooth. At any point when my eyelids had the audacity to even try and close, a bump in the road would send the minivan lurching from side to side and I would be jolted awake again. It was with my eyes firmly open, therefore, that we headed deep into the countryside.

Whilst the weather was far from tropical and summer was clearly a long way off, the first shoots of spring were visible as we wound through the country. There were still several large coverings of snow, but these were confined to the higher points of some of the surrounding hills. On the lower slopes the slightest tinges of green were beginning to appear and give colour to the previously bleak landscape. However, whilst the countryside was clearly getting ready for spring, the same could not be said for the area's tourist facilities, the majority of which remained firmly in hibernation. Their operators were obviously waiting for temperatures to rise a little more, for the spring thaw to completely set in and for more than one van-load of foreigners to arrive before they opened their gates. This left us driving around the park in a desperate search for somewhere to stay.

We passed several camps which were well populated with gers or log cabins, but were also bereft of human life. I was particularly disappointed when we passed one that boasted a collection of almost life-sized plastic dinosaurs scattered amongst the accommodation. Unfortunately, no matter how much fun sliding down the tail of a brontosaurus – a la Fred Flintstone – would have been, the gates to the camp were chained closed and we had to settle for a different one a few kilometres down the road.

Whilst the camp we were forced to plump for was lacking a mini dinosaur park, it was circled by some impressive hills, which would be perfect for hiking. Once we had sorted out two gers for the night, we decided it was time to explore the countryside. As soon as we arrived Mitch, Ryan, Fran and I had spotted an imposing hill about a kilometre away, which looked intimidating enough to be worth tackling. With it firmly in our sights we filled our water bottles and set off towards the base. Once we had crossed a rickety wooden bridge, we found ourselves on the banks of a relatively wide and fast flowing river.

Our chances of crossing did not look good. It was almost twenty meters to the far bank, the water looked way too deep to wade across and there was no bridge in sight. After spending months cursing the ice and snow in UB, we appeared to have, quiet ironically, fallen foul of the warm spring weather. In winter, the water would have been frozen, whilst in summer the stream would be far shallower and the current far less strong. However, in mid April, the whole river was flush with thawed snow that had melted its way down from the adjacent hills.

The river looked intimidating, but we didn't want to give in easily. Instead, we went in search of some locals who may have been able to help us to get across. We managed to find two guys dressed in dels standing by their horses, who informed us that the nearest bridge was half way back to Ulaan Baatar and that the only way across was on horseback. They offered to take us across on the horses they had with them. However, we were deterred by the fact that they refused to promise to come pick us up later in the day and the prospect of being stranded on the opposite bank to our ger was not an appealing one.

With the river putting a premature end to our first expedition, we decided to opt for plan B and aim for a smaller, tree covered hill back on our side of the river. The approach to the new hill was far less steep than the one across the valley. We began our ascent by crossing a boggy field close to our ger, before heading up a gentle incline covered by almost skeletal looking trees. Once we had left the ger and the surrounding camp behind us, almost every trace of greenery seemed to vanish and our walk took on a somewhat ghostly feel. The trees looked frighteningly thin and lifeless whilst the ground on which we trod was two to three inches deep in autumnal looking pine needles that offered a soft orange carpet underfoot.

As eerie as the early stages of our climb were, the conditions made for pretty easy progress. The lack of greenery allowed us to pick an easy path towards the summit and the rich pile of needles on the ground ensured it was supremely easy going on our feet. However, as we got higher that began to change. The trees gradually began to thin out before disappearing completely and the carpet of pine needles gave way to jaggy rocks dusted with a faint covering of snow.

As we reached the summit, we found ourselves breathless thanks to a combination of the heavy walking we had just done and the scenery that was on show all around us. In one direction we looked across at the hill we were unable to tackle and then beyond it, down a long sweeping valley that disappeared into the distance.

Then, in another, we could stare back in the direction of UB past a series of hills, all covered in the same sort of skeletal woodland as our own. Looking away from the capital city we saw yet more rolling hills and another valley that swept away out of sight. The four of us sat on the jagged rocks that signified the peak of the hill and basked in the stunning sights that encircled us. The howling wind blocked out almost any background noise there would have been, leaving us to enjoy the view in near complete peace. It was glorious.

We basked for almost an hour before taking some spectacular photographs then deciding it was time to head back to the bottom. The return leg of the trip proved far easier on the calves as we ambled down the slope at leisure. However, some of the rocks proved far trickier to negotiate on the way down, making for slow progress at times. Thanks to this slackened pace it took us almost as long to reach the bottom, as it had to get to the top. Unlike our quest for the summit though, we had the comforts of a ger waiting for us as we headed down the hillside.

A night in a ger

Our ger had five beds positioned around its circumference. Just as was the case at Grandpa's home in UB, there was a large stove at the centre with a pipe that rose out through a hole in the top of the cone shaped roof. Once the stove was put to use, wood-smoke began to billow out into the evening sky and our circular home for the evening warmed up rapidly. Before we had set-off to Terelje I was dubious as to how warm some felt wrapped around a few sticks could actually keep us during a cold Mongolian night. Consequently, I had taken my sleeping bag, thermals and several layers of clothing to sleep in. However, as it transpired, I was to be tremendously and very pleasantly surprised. The felt acted as a superb insulator keeping almost all the warmth generated by the stove from escaping into the night. Because of this, not only were my thermals and extra layers left redundant, but I found myself breaking into a sweat whilst wearing just the shorts and t-shirt I would ordinarily have slept in at the Batmunkh's centrally-heated apartment.

Having chatted and played cards until the light outside had completely dissipated, we used the warm atmosphere of the ger to drift off to sleep. As I closed my eyes, my surroundings were toasty warm. However when I opened them again nine hours later the temperature had dropped dramatically. We had made the rookie mistake of letting the fire in the stove burn out and, in so doing, allowed the cold to creep in from outside. Therefore, our first task of the morning was to stock the stove with wood and get the fire burning. Once smoke was puffing up through the chimney-pipe and out into the fresh morning sky, we could warm up and then tuck into a breakfast of instant noodles, bread and cookies.

After we had polished off our meal, it was time to get the second half of the weekend under way and saddle up for some horse-trekking. Mongolia is famous in equine circles for the unique breed of horse that roams its countryside and once carried Chinggis Khan and his armies across Asia and into Europe and the Far East. In the west, they are known as the Przewalski horse, a name they acquired thanks to the Russian naturalist who was the first westerner to set eyes on one in its natural habitat – the residents of Eastern Europe saw plenty of them when Chinggis was on the rampage.

The Przewalski differ from horses in the rest of the world because of their shaggy manes and diminutive stature. A fully grown adult male is barely half the size of a regular horse and boasts a mane that is not only visually striking, but also offers the rider an excellent place to grip in case of emergency. They can carry a rider and baggage for up to 60km a day, which has made them a valuable commodity throughout Mongolian history.

There are hundreds of the famous Mongolian horses in Terelje helping their owners make a living both through a traditional herding role and also as tourist attractions. As soon as we mentioned to the owner of our ger camp that we were looking to find some horses for the afternoon, we were surrounded by scores of locals thrusting the reins of their horses into our hands. It took several minutes gesticulating and arguing – with the much-needed assistance of a passing English speaker – for us to agree on the renting of the horses and an appropriate price. We presumed that would have been the hard part, but we could not have been more wrong. Getting ten novices onto their horses all at once proved to be no easy feat. Several of us struggled to get up and seated, whilst those that did faced difficulties in stopping their horses from ambling off in random directions. Eventually, after thirty rather frenzied minutes we were all in the saddle and ready to move out.

Mongolians ride their horses with the use of a very small wooden saddle, which as soon as I mounted my horse, I found tremendously uncomfortable. No matter how I adjusted my legs or buttocks, it still seemed to be causing me some rather intimate discomfort. However, regardless of the uncomfortable riding conditions, I soon began to love my horse-bound experience. Once we had rode away from the ger, we were able to head in the direction away from UB and explore the sweeping valley we had seen from the hilltop the previous day.

We maintained a sedate pace at first taking in the scenery and getting comfortable in the saddle. As we moved onto the valley floor, the trees around our ger camp fell away and we were greeted by a panoramic blue sky. With the wide horizon up ahead and the horse swaying beneath me, I was instantly put in mind of old-fashioned westerns in which I had seen such scenery. I quickly began to imagine myself as Alan Ladd in Shane or John Wayne in countless other movies of the same ilk.

Truth-be-told, despite my illusions and the Hank Williams soundtrack playing across my mind, we looked like the sorriest posse ever to take the reins. Even though I had purchased a cowboy-style hat back in Ulaan Baatar, my sneakers and waterproof jacket were garments no self-respecting cattle rustler would ever have been seen dead in. Similarly, one of the girls was wearing a pink woolly hat that didn't quite fit in with the wild-west motif either. It was still great fun though!

After thirty minutes and just over a mile of riding, I began to feel that I had got the hang of the whole horsemanship lark. I was no longer being thrown around uncomfortably in the saddle and I was managing to head in a straight line at a relatively sedate but nevertheless controlled speed. Ryan and I were blazing a trail at the front of the group and soon decided that it was time to put our newly found confidence to the test. I gave my horse a gentle nudge in the ribs and he responded by accelerating his pace. Ryan followed suit and we were soon moving away at a trot and then a canter.

Up until then, the ride had been interesting but not especially thrilling. As soon as we went up a gear though, the excitement levels followed suit. Where my horse had previously chosen his steps carefully and deftly navigated his way around any minor obstacles, he was suddenly far less discriminate in placing his hooves and even made the odd little hop over things in his path. We seemed to get faster with each step and, as we did so, I seriously began to contemplate a life out on the steppe, spending my days on horseback and my nights in a ger.

It wasn't until we had reached the far end of the valley and then circled back towards our camp that I started to realize how riding a Mongolian horse was not the cakewalk I was imagining it to be and could, in fact, take quite the physical toll on an unprepared rider. As we trotted in the direction of our ger, I began to feel a little stiffness in my inner thighs. By the time we were within touching distance of our camp, the stiffness had become full-on pain and had spread as far as my ankles. After I dismounted it seemed as though my feet were three feet apart, making walking uncomfortable in the extreme.

10. ICE COLD IN TOV AIMAG

The weekend of hiking and horse trekking in Terelje had given us our first taste of what the freshly thawed Mongolian countryside had to offer. The sweeping valleys, expansive greenery and uncontained skies had whetted our appetite for the great outdoors. Our night in the ger had also given us a taste for getting just that little bit closer to nature. To satisfy this urge, we began to plan an ambitious camping expedition to Manzshir Khiid, a ruined monastery in Tov aimag about 45 kilometres south-east of Ulaan Baatar. Our plan was to blend our desire to get out into the Mongolian countryside with a little history and culture.

The monastery at Manzshir Khhid was originally founded in 1773 and named after Manjushri, the Buddha of Wisdom. At its peak, in the 1800s, it was home to over 350 monks living in twenty buildings. Perhaps unsurprisingly, though, along with so many other temples and shrines, it was destroyed in the purges of the 1930s by Choibalsan and his henchmen. It has since been restored, but in no way measures up to its previous size or beauty. However, after conferring with Shawn during a prolonged newsroom lull and consulting my rather battered copy of Lonely Planet, we learned that some of the ruins that had been left behind by the Communist bulldozers were quite majestic in themselves. Apparently, they were set dramatically at the end of a long valley and at the foot of an imposing cliff face, which served to capture a wonderful combination of nature and spirituality. Not only that, but the cliffs were home to some colourful Buddhist cave paintings that had survived the Communists.

The temple was also recommended as an approach route to one of Mongolia's most impressive peaks, Tsetseegum Uul. The mountain, which measures 2260m, is the highest in the Bogdkhan Uul range that dominates the skyline to the south of Ulaan Baatar. Tsetseegum, along with Chingeltei, Songino Khairkhan and Bayanzurkh, rises above the remainder of the range with the four of them referred to as the Holy Peaks by locals. The towering group roughly corresponds to the four points on a compass and are accepted as one of the best areas in which to explore the wilder regions surrounding the capital city.

Tsetseegum can be attacked from four major routes with the approach from Manzshir Khiid reputed to be the easiest and most accessible. From the summit, most estimates suggested that the outlying districts of the city were a ten-hour hike away and recommended an overnight camp to make the journey manageable. With our new wanderlust pushing us forward, we began to make plans to go visit Manzshir Khiid and then hike our way back to the city.

Out into the country

Our plan was to arrive at Manzshir Khiid on the Friday evening, camp there overnight and then tackle Tsetseegum Uul the next morning. From there, we would make our way through the mountain range towards the city, pitching our tents once we ran out of light. This all sounded very simple and straightforward to us. However, the plans met with a great deal of scepticism from almost everyone we divulged them to. The other i-to-i volunteers, the regulars at Steppe Inn, the staff at the UB Post and the writers of Lonely Planet all thought the weather would be far too cold for us. The guidebook described the trip as: "only sensible from July". However, despite the many doubters, no one was going to stop us from putting our tents to use. Fran and Mitch had specifically bought a bright blue piece of Chinese camping technology and I had not lugged my tent in my baggage all the way from Sheffield via London and Moscow to Ulaan Baatar, for it to sit dormant on the floor of my room. Naturally, we did take some heed of the warnings we had been given. So, we made sure we were well prepared. We stocked up by purchasing insulated mats, skewers for cooking, bottled water and as much tinned food as we could comfortably carry. And, of course, we packed plenty of warm clothing.

When Friday evening came around, we piled the supplies along with our packs into the back of the jeep we had hired and set off towards Tov. Manzshir Khiid is a couple of miles north of the town of Zunmod. From there, the road looped back and headed into the mountains. As we entered the Bogdkhan National Park, we weaved in and out of several wooded peaks before entering the valley that housed our destination. As we zipped over the grassland, along the side of the dirt-road we began to see scores of marmots happily burrowing in the earth, which we thought were a fantastic sight and soon had us in deep conversation about some of the stories we had heard about the creatures.

Mongolia is home to the *Marmota sibirica* or the Mongolian Marmot, known to locals as Tarvaga. They hibernate for six months a year. So, presumably, we were viewing them only a few weeks after their winter sleep. They were cute little creatures, but we were also acutely aware that many of them still carry bubonic plague. So, we gave them a wide berth.

Marmots are heavily hunted in Mongolia. They are prized for their meat and oil, whilst their fur is also often exported for sale in Russia. Hunting techniques vary, but according to several sources - including a spectacularly drunken Englishman at Steppe Inn - one of the most popular is to camouflage oneself in floppy rabbit-like ears and flowing white clothing and to dance around manically in front of them. Apparently, the dazzled marmots then stand to attention completely mesmerised by the entire effect. This obviously makes them far easier to shoot or club than when they are aware enough to simply run away. It didn't seem a particularly sporting technique to me. I must admit, though, that it sounded a rather fun approach to hunting.

We also learned that many herdsmen hunt marmots for food and consider them quite the delicacy. After shooting the marmot, the herdsmen take the rather gory approach of skinning, gutting and filleting the animal before turning the skin inside out to form a kind of bag, into which the marmot meat is placed. They then cook the meat inside the skin over an open fire.

The marmots, though, were the least of our concerns when we reached Manzshir Khiid. We needed to find a camp-site, pitch our tents, make a fire and cook some food before we lost the quickly fading light. We unloaded everything from the jeep and bade farewell to our driver, who headed back to UB. We then made our way west to find ourselves a sheltered locale in the woods where we could camp for the night.

We hiked for a mile up some steep hills before coming upon a series of small clearings in the trees. The first of these was a no-go as the earth was frozen and tent pegs would sink barely a centimetre into the ground (This was not a good omen for the coming night). So, we moved further along and found the second of the clearings. The ground took a peg easily and we were offered shelter by trees on three sides. So, we decided to pitch up for the night.

My tent proved to be one of the most complex pieces of technology I have ever seen. It had seemed easy to use in the camping store in Sheffield when I bought it, but out in the wild it proved to be horrifically confusing. Whilst Fran and Mitch threw their Chinese version together in a matter of minutes, Ryan and I were left puzzling over tension bands inner layers, outer layers, fly sheets and three different sizes of peg. As a result of this Mitch and Fran had the fire well on its way by the time our green tent was finally standing.

Wrestling with tents can soon create an appetite. So, we all dived into the woods to find as much dry wood as possible to stoke the fire enough to cook. Our meal of hot-dog sausages and toasted sweet breads probably wasn't up to the standards of UB's top lunch spots. It didn't even compare all that favourably to Oyuna's home cooking. But, nevertheless, it was hearty fare and we tucked in eagerly. The expedition seemed to be going well as we donned our thermals, fastened our tents and zipped up our sleeping bags for our first night in the wilderness.

A very cold night

It wasn't the most comfortable sleeping situation ever. The ground was hard and wasn't super warm. But, once I had got wrapped up warm and snuggled down into my sleeping bag, it seemed like it would be ok. It wouldn't! Things started to take a turn for the worse at around 3am, when the uncomfortable cold woke me with a jolt and a shiver. I quickly delved into my bag to unearth as much extra clothing as possible. This was far from an easy task in a shallow two-man tent that also housed our packs and food. The resultant rustling was loud enough to wake Ryan, Mitch, Fran and any nearby marmots who had not yet come out of hibernation. Once I had added some much needed layers and wrapped up as warm as possible we all tried to get some sleep. However, the cold would soon strike again.

It was approaching 6 am when the first chinks of light began to seep through the fly sheet along with the sound of Mitch bemoaning the poor quality of the tent, his sleeping bag and everything else that was failing to keep him warm. As disturbing as this noise was, he had a point. None of us could profess to being truly warm and we were beginning to appreciate the opinions of those who had warned us against our foolhardy project.

The forest floor appeared to have frozen overnight as the cold crept in. The wind was also whistling through the pine trees and putting the tension bands on my tent to the test. I sat in my sleeping-bag with my head poking through the door to my tent enjoying a drink of newly chilled bottled water. As I did so, I began to question the wisdom both in our choice of camp-site and in the expedition as a whole.

At 6 am on a bitingly cold morning, there was nothing else to do but get on with things. We restarted the fire, but it seemed to make precious little difference to our core temperatures. We all sat shivering and feeling genuinely glum Despite all my western clothing and camping equipment, the Mongolian weather and countryside still left me unfathomably cold. We had a quick and 'nutritious' breakfast of toasted bread and Haribo candies before we decided to make our way to the ruins of the monastery and see what they had to offer.

The synopses we had received prior to our trip were correct, the ruins were nothing spectacular in themselves, but captured the imagination because of their setting. They were surrounded by mountains to either side and were sat at the bottom of an impressive cliff face. The valley which led up to it undulated like waves that lapped against the rubble of the ancient monastery. Everything was, of course, also deeply silent. It all worked really well to create a great sense of spirituality.

It was a beautiful sight. For a few minutes, the scenery succeeded in taking our minds of the cold, which came as a blessed relief. We spent a good 30 minutes or so drinking in the silence, the serenity and historical significance of the spot before we began to contemplate beginning our journey back to UB. The cliffs that stood before us seemed to be almost vertical, but we had no option other than to climb them. The only way back to UB was to scale the cliff and continue north.

The cliffs proved to be quite a climb. With our large packs, we made slow and tottery progress as we inched up the almost vertical face. Once we had got over the top, though, we found ourselves on the trail that led to Tsetseegum. It was a frustrating period as we wandered past several locations that offered fantastic shelter and may well have afforded us a far warmer night's sleep.

For the majority of the way, it was a warm day and we were walking on a firm, but at times unfrozen, track that wound between trees and giant boulders. We followed the trail, but continually checked with our compasses that we were heading predominantly north and a touch west. Just before lunchtime, we came out of the trees and were in sight of the summit. For the final few hundred yards of our ascent, we had to traverse a boggy meadow before scaling a series of large slab like boulders that led to a small plateau. At 2260m the air was decidedly colder and we were being whipped by some harsh winds. So, in the lee of some large rocks a 50m or so away from the summit, we hunkered down for lunch – cold hot-dog sausages. They did not match our meal the previous evening, but gave us some much needed energy after our morning's exertions.

All morning, as we hiked upwards, we had been debating what we should do that evening. We may have had the appropriate equipment and enough food to manage another night in the cold, but it was far from an ideal scenario. The idea began to float between the four of us that we could head on at speed, make UB before sunset and not be forced to spend another night in our tents.

My thoughts on the matter were split. I was disappointed at the idea of going back early and not maximising my wilderness experience, but, on the other hand, I had been woken by the sheer cold the previous night and was not keen on repeating such an experience. The whole group felt a similar way. We were genuinely torn between the romance of our expedition and the practicalities of being just too damn cold. However, from the summit of Tsetseegum the warmth of Ulaan Baatar was still up to ten hours away according to most sources. So, it was by no means certain that we would even get close to the city before the light gave way.

Once we had reached Tsetseegum's blustery peak, we put thoughts of the journey home to the back of our minds for just a few moments. The windswept panorama was spectacular. It took in rolling hills, snow capped peaks and the city way off in the distance. It was an exhilarating experience to simply breathe in the fresh mountain air and gaze at the awe-inspiring mountain scenery. However, we quickly came down to earth when we focused on just how far away UB was.

The distance was exacerbated by the knowledge that the terrain between the comfort of our respective apartments and ourselves was far harsher than what we had covered already. It was widely accepted that the route down the mountain via Zaisan was the hardest approach to Tsetseegum and was littered with vast fields of boulders. Like all the previous warnings we had received for our trip, we ignored this one too and decided to press on regardless of the hostile terrain. After much soul-searching we had decided that our plan was to try to get to UB before sunrise and only camp if we absolutely, positively had to. We questioned how bad it could actually be, especially as we were going downhill. We would find out quickly.

The long march home

Once away from the summit, we hit some dense woodland and were forced to painstakingly weave our way through the trees and down the incline. The chilly temperatures of the early morning had risen away and the biting winds that whistled across Tsetseegum abated as we descended, leaving it almost perfect hiking weather. The first hour's progress was relatively serene as we hopped over the soft woodland floor. Our problems started when we began to encounter the first of the many fields of boulders.

The vast expanse was made up of stones that were up to six feet in length and almost as much in width. At first, it was rather fun leaping between each rock a step at a time. However, with large backpacks containing camping equipment that was weighing us down, it made for a precarious process. It was fortunate that the snows had melted and that no rain had fallen, otherwise it would have been unlikely we'd have escaped without one or two broken ankles at the very least. Dealing with the boulders would soon get very old.

It took us several hours to battle through the boulders. They were large, they were precarious and they just wouldn't seem to go away. It was like a nightmare from which we could not awake. Each time we thought we had woken up, we would be dragged back into a ghastly slumber. Every time we reached a patch of soft woodland floor, we hoped we were free from their vicious grip and were about to enjoy a prolonged period of even ground. Yet, it seemed that our hopes were continuously being dashed as we would find yet another field sat in our path just a few hundred metres later.

As the afternoon drew on, we began to lose our bearings slightly. Ulaan Baatar was eclipsed from our view by the woods and hills that lay in front of us. Coupled with this our compasses began to offer some erratic readings. To afford ourselves some insurance we had taken two, the most accurate of which was the one Fran had brought from England. Mine was made in Mongolia, purchased from the State Department Store and offered a variable interpretation of which direction was north.

As we battled field after field of giant boulders – with our energy and motivation levels dropping by the minute – we began to get extremely nervous that we had lost our direction and were wandering in circles. We presumed the array of rocks had something to do with the spinning needle of my compass. So, we headed in the vague direction of north and hoped we were on track.

When we finally negotiated our way through the rocks and back on to the soft forest floor, our compasses again gave some relatively accurate pointers. Fortunately, we were only ten or fifteen degrees out and were still on track to make UB by sunset. It just became a race against time. We needed to get back to the city before the sun dropped below the horizon. We were all relieved to have negotiated our way through the rocks with only a couple of minor trips and bumps. The fields of boulders had been so dense and continued for so long that as we began to near Ulaan Baatar we still daren't let ourselves believe they were finished. All the false dawns we had encountered made us question whether we were genuinely free from our knee-scraping, foot-aching recurring dream.

We realised that to reach the city we had to emerge from the wooded hills somewhere close to the Zaisan memorial. This was relatively simple. However, we also knew that we had to avoid stepping into the valley reserved for the presidential residence, which was about 3km away from Zaisan. As fun as dropping in on President Bagabandi would have been, it was not unknown for western hikers to be detained for long periods of time for an accidental trespass. The last thing we needed after such an arduous hike was to be mistaken for foreign intelligence operatives and detained for questioning.

Thankfully, we managed to get our navigation correct. We finished our descent from Tsetseegum through a valley approximately one kilometre east of the president's residence. Instead of the Bagabandi's guards all we came across was a farm defended by a vociferous but largely toothless dog.

At around six in the evening, we hit the first of the roads that led back into the city - we had made it back with a clear two hours of daylight left. Despite the blisters inside our boots and our sore shoulders, there was a great sense of achievement, especially in light of all those sensible individuals who had called our idea ridiculous. A little cold and a few scrapes hadn't hurt us too much. All that was left was to take the road back into the city. It ran parallel to Peace Avenue, but was separated from the city by the river and five kilometres of wasteland. As we trudged back along it we passed Bagabandi's bachelor pad from the outside. The vast white building was tucked between two hills and set back from the road by about two kilometres. It was an impressive home for a man who at best could be described as a two-bit semi-dictator. The majority of his nation lives either in crowded, dilapidated apartment blocks or in felt covered gers that barely keep out the harsh weather.

11. THE ODYSSEY

When May came around, my tenure at the UB Post came to an end and I got my chance to explore Mongolia on a wider scale. However, before I bade my farewell to the paper and staff, I was given yet another chance to add to the nation's escalating alcohol statistics when I was thrown a late night leaving party at which we sampled vodka in a traditional Mongolian style. The entire team sat around the main table in the newsroom and each drank from the same mug. The drink began its journey with the most senior person present, our editor-in-chief Oyunbayar, before visiting Sumya, Uyanga and then the rest of us.

Even though the rest of the staff and I were a long way removed from some of the comatose drunks you could see on the street, we had soon emptied two litre bottles of Kharaa vodka. So, Batmunkh and Sumya were dispatched to the local store for extra supplies. A 3am finale and a splitting headache the next morning made for a fitting end to my journalistic career in Mongolia.

My departure from three months living with the Batmunkhs was less spectacular, but went along similar lines. I had spent my final Friday evening in UB at Steppe Inn and then at a house party somewhere downtown. Because of this, I was spending my final Saturday morning nursing a queasy stomach and pounding head. I was making some rather slow and ineffectual attempts at packing when Oyuna entered my room unannounced and beckoned me through to the family's living room. Inside, the table was laid out with buuz, sausage, orange juice and, unsurprisingly, vodka.

Since it was my final day with the family, there was no chance whatsoever of me refusing the vodka, no matter how delicate my stomach was feeling. So I, Oyuna and Batmunkh worked our way through a giant plate of buuz and well into the vodka. With my stomach in the state it was, that was no mean feat. If it weren't for the presence of the orange juice as a much needed chaser I may well have embarrassed myself by having to vomit during my final breakfast.

Before I left for good, we exchanged typically Mongolian parting gifts. The family handed me a large bottle of Chinggis Khan Vodka and I reciprocated with a bottle of scotch for Batmunkh and Oyuna and some cake for the children. Once we had left the bowl of buuz containing nothing more than a puddle of mutton fat and the bottle holding only a few drops of vodka, I said "Sayora" and made my break for the road.

UB - Moron

It was late Sunday afternoon when Fran, Mitch and I met up

182

ready for our last and most ambitious expedition in Mongolia. Our destination was Khovsgol Nuur, one of Mongolia's greatest natural assets and, simultaneously, one of the most remote and challenging sights in all of Asia. It is known as the 'Dark Blue Pearl of Mongolia' and stretches 136km in length and 36km in width. These dimensions make it the fourteenth largest freshwater lake on earth, representing 1% of the planet's fresh water. We were aware that we had not chosen the best time of year to visit since the lake was generally frozen until well into May and often into June as well. Nevertheless, our time in the country was running out fast, so it was a case of now or never when we caught our train on a balmy Saturday evening.

The train leg of our journey took fourteen hours and wound through the cold dark night and was broken only by a two-hour stopover in Darkhan during the very early hours of the morning. From there, we travelled a further 183km to Erdenet. The city at the end of the first leg of our journey was Mongolia's key industrial hub, home to the Erdenet Mining Corporation - a joint venture between Mongolia and Russia that produces 25 million tonnes of ore each year to help sustain the faltering Mongolian economy.

The sun began to pour through the wafer thin Trans-Mongolian Railway curtains at just before 7am. The delicate morning light showed that the approaches to Erdenet were cluttered with mining works and heavy industry. These sights were pretty uninspiring, but when we noticed the ample covering of snow that rested on them we were quickly raised from our state of semi-slumber. There had been no new snow in Ulaan Baatar for almost a month and we had been walking around in T-shirts and jeans. Suddenly we were being flung back two months – we were back to needing layer upon layer of clothes and to the greying snow we all hoped that we had escaped forever.

As the train drew to a halt, we were rifling through our bags for thermals, gloves, hats and all the apparel we had used in winter. I had included mine merely as an emergency measure and had never expected to be wearing them so soon into our trip. However, when we stepped onto the windswept, bitingly cold platform I was immeasurably glad I had stuffed them into the bottom of my rucksack.

Possibly the most pertinent description of the scenery in and around Erdenet is "bleak". When we dismounted from the train we were greeted by a greyish landscape dotted with darkened apartment blocks and more mining works. However, Erdenet wasn't on the schedule for its scenic potential. It was the only place from where we could get transport to either Bulgan or Moron, the two potential next steps on our journey. Bulgan was the closer of the two options, a mere sixty kilometres and three hours by jeep away. Moron, on the other hand, was almost 400 kilometres away and would involve an overnight journey by minivan. Having only just completed a fourteen-hour train journey, a trip of such proportions seemed less than inviting.

Even though we were leaning towards heading to Bulgan anyway, our decision was made for us by the scarcity of transport options. It was a cold, dark Monday morning in Erdenet and the only jeep or minivan we could find was headed for Bulgan there and then. It became a case of either take it or stand around in the cold and wait for other options that may never come. So, without having seen too much of Erdenet or having had any breakfast, we took the only option on offer and piled our gear into the back.

The ride to Bulgan was decidedly claustrophobic. Fran, Mitch and I were stuffed into the back seat alongside a middle-aged herdsman. The front seat was equally crowded, with the driver, a man in the passenger seat and a teenage boy all wedged in. With such weight in the vehicle, we set off westwards at a very slow pace. Despite only creeping away from Erdenet we were soon off the paved roads and heading across the interweaving array of dirt tracks that make up Mongolia's highways. The journey was similar to our jaunt across the steppe on our wolf hunting expedition. Just as then, I was being thrown around the vehicle with my head bouncing against the roof and windows at regular intervals.

After three squashed, slightly sweaty hours, we finally rumbled and swayed our way into Bulgan. We managed to locate the only hotel in town and found ourselves a room with four beds, plenty of dust, a broken shower and very little heating. As unwelcoming and uncomfortable as our 'suite' was, it was home for the day. So, with our bags stowed, we decided it was time to eat.

Our quest for a hot meal followed a similar pattern to that at our hotel in Sainshand several weeks earlier. The menu in the restaurant next door exhibited a wide variety of hearty Mongolia food, which, after seventeen hours of travelling sustained on nothing more than candy and instant noodles, was much needed. However, just as in the Gobi we were disappointed. There was in-fact only one meal that was actually available. In southern Mongolia we managed a plate of Tsuiven; in the north we were supplied with a plate of mutton and gravy alongside a serving of cold rice.

As dull as our meal was, it probably ranked as the most exciting thing about Bulgan. The town amounted to little more than a solitary paved street containing a few shacks and general stores. It took us little more than fifteen minutes to walk from one end of the street to the other and back to the hotel. With so little entertainment on offer, we decided there was nothing else for it but to retire to our room and contribute to the local alcohol statistics.

We woke early the next morning to get a jeep to Moron and, if we were lucky, on to Khatgal – the small town at the base of Lake Khovsgol. It was a clear but chilly day, perfect for heading out across the steppe. The jeep station was crammed with vehicles, but unfortunately, because it was so early in the year, not too many of the drivers were prepared to take us such a long distance. In fact, the only man to step forward was a larger than life character named Oyga, who was around five and a half feet tall and maybe just as wide. His face was a deep red colour and was garnished with the odd burst capillary that made it look as though he could collapse from a heart attack at any point. Nevertheless, he owned a jeep and was prepared to take us as far as we wanted to go.

Our objective at the start of the day was to reach Khatgal. However, the journey was approaching 500 km across rough terrain, which meant our initial plan was probably a touch optimistic. After a process of lengthy negotiations, during which our inability to speak Mongolian seriously hindered us, we managed to agree to a slightly elevated price of Tg125,000 (just less than 100USD). We had been hoping to pay far less for the privilege of traversing a large tract of Mongolian countryside, but Oyga was adamant that because it was so early in the year he would be unable to find any passengers for his return trip and therefore we would have to pay for his petrol to get home. So, with no other choice, we loaded our bags into the back of his white jeep and began our journey.

Once we had set off, we managed to get as far as the centre of town before our progress was cut short. Oyga drew up outside a wooden shack, killed the engine and got out, leaving the three of us sitting there in a state of bewilderment whilst he disappeared inside. Around ten minutes later he re-emerged next to a stout, thickset lady who was carrying a dustpan, brush and a large flask. She opened the door to the jeep and began sweeping around our feet, she then thrust the flask into Oyga's arms and pushed him into the driver's seat. It was pretty clear that our driver couldn't make the overnight trip without okaying it with the missus, which gave us all a little chuckle.

It was mid-morning by the time we eventually hit the road out of town in earnest. Our progress for the first few kilometres was serene as we glided over a paved road that was winding through the hills surrounding Bulgan. However, it was no surprise when after just a few miles the road began to get bumpier, before petering away to nothing more than a dirt track. The scenery along the way was absolutely stunning and completely unabridged. The hills rolled from horizon to horizon and beyond with the only signs of life coming in the shape of the telephone wires by which Oyga was navigating – with no roads and few towns, maps were not really all that well used in Mongolia.

After traversing such sparse and eye-catching countryside for almost three hours, our solitary drive led us to a collection of shabby looking huts that served as the best and only eatery for miles around. It was here that our hopes of making Khatgal that night, which had already been looking slim, were completely scuppered by Oyga's voracious appetite. We would have been happy with just a bowl of mutton soup for our late lunch, but our amply proportioned driver insisted that we stay for two courses of mutton servings, along with several bowls of salty milk – a local delicacy. Whilst Oyga slurped and chomped his way through a lunch large enough to feed three regularly sized men, we sat idle whilst valuable travelling time ticked away. No amount of tutting and judgy British stares could shift him!

Eventually, we managed to drag our driver away from the food and back into his vehicle. However, despite a hard afternoon's driving we failed to even reach Moron by sundown and, as the last embers of the sun faded out, the dirt tracks over which we were travelling became more and more treacherous by the second. Oyga could not see too far in front of his own face ensuring that every now and again we would hit a bump or bounce into a hole that would send us careering across the back seat or lurching forward towards the wind-shield.

Whilst we were making such fraught progress, I began to get a touch concerned that Oyga clearly couldn't carry on in these conditions for too long and that we might well find ourselves stranded out in the wilderness. The prospect of sleeping in the jeep was not one that was filling me with either warmth or excitement and I began getting uncomfortable flashbacks to the cold early morning we struggled through at Manzshir Khiid. Thankfully, about forty minutes after the sun went down, we finally began to sight the distant lights of a remote town. We rolled into Moron about twenty minutes later and began our search for somewhere to stay.

Moron-Khatgal

After a night in a typically dirty and cold hotel room, we headed for breakfast and our second incredulously large meal with Oyga. We managed to find a guanz (small cafe) where we ordered noodle soup followed by a portion of mutton, rice and gravy. During the first course, the three of us were cutting away large lumps of fat from the small pieces of mutton that were floating in the soup and leaving the greasy white lumps on the side of our bowls. To us, it was unhealthy and a bit disgusting. Oyga, on the other hand, was cutting away the meat and chomping down on the large lumps of fat with glee. We seemed to be gaining something of an insight into why he boasted the physique he did. Not only did he eat his own fat, but he then devoured ours as well.

With our hearty breakfast and Oyga's ventricle threateningly heartier one tucked away, we stopped off to stock up on supplies for the final leg of our journey. We piled in everyday staples like water, noodles and bread, but also decided to slip in one other Mongolian necessity – vodka. We were on a road trip, so we figured we should get in the mood! The boxed up supplies were slotted on top of our rucksacks in the rear of the jeep and then we set off for another day's driving.

Yet again, it was not long before we had exhausted the paved roads and were following the telephone wires across the steppe once more. However, we had not gone far when Oyga drew the jeep to a halt in what appeared to be the middle of nowhere. To our bemusement he began to unscrew the courtesy light in the roof and then pointed excitedly at our shopping. Apparently, he had spotted the vodka we had slipped in and was very keen to sample some. Again, saying no to a Mongolian with the sniff of vodka in his nostrils proved to be impossible. So, we passed the bottle forward for him to open.

Once the drink was cracked, the light became an impromptu shot glass with Oyga grasping it first and chugging down a large shot. Then, just as at my leaving party a few days previously, the glass was passed around the group of us with each of us taking a drink before Oyga finished what was left. He then screwed the cover back on his light, threw the bottle onto the previously unspoiled steppe and set off towards Khatgal.

Tuesday's drive was a far less epic undertaking, lasting only three hours. It was just after lunchtime when we crossed a wooden bridge over the Khatgal River and entered a wind-swept town of log cabins that seemed to be lacking any form of human life. We drove around aimlessly for about twenty minutes looking for signs of life before we came across two teenage guys sitting outside the local store. Fortunately, one of them spoke a little English and agreed to help us find a place to stay.

In summer, Khatgal is relatively well populated with backpackers and the occasional Korean tourist. They are all in search of stunning scenery, wild horse trekking and epic hiking. However, in winter and well into spring the lake is frozen, temperatures are low and the area attracts far fewer visitors. Because of the seasonal disparity, later in the year the town is surrounded by an array of ger camps that offer solar showers and warm beds. In May, however, these camps remained closed and we were left struggling to locate anywhere to sleep. Our only option turned out to be a ger that was ordinarily home to the town's harbour-master, who was prepared to move out and stay with his family whilst we were in town.

The arrival of the first westerners for months was big news around Khatgal and spread like wildfire. The town's doctor and a local herdsman cum tour guide named Ochirbaat or Ochi for short soon joined the little group in our ger. Yet again, a bottle of vodka was opened and a glass was passed around our circular accommodation. The curiosity and vodka drinking carried on for most of the afternoon with Oyga showing little interest in heading back to his wife in Bulgan – he was clearly enjoying the freedom.

It eventually took a couple of hours, some not so subtle hints and a serious depletion in the level of vodka for us to be granted some privacy. The harbour-master headed over to his family's cabin, Ochi headed back to his home-stay and Oyga departed into town in search of more vodka. We were left with just one remaining guest – the town's doctor.

Khatgal's top physician had enjoyed a good long drink and had fallen comatose across my bed. As much as we tried, we could neither move nor rouse him. Each time we shook him he would grunt, throw his arms into the air and fall into an even deeper sleep. This left the three of us worrying that we may have had an unwanted overnight guest. However, his incessant and deafening snoring convinced us that we could not allow him to spend the night. Instead, we sought the harbour-master's assistance in removing him.

Our host's approach was simple and, truth-be-told, a touch violent. He began with a few gentle nudges that progressed into a firm shake then a series of slaps across the face. Once the inert medic eventually came back to life, the harbour-master regained his sensitive side, taking him by the arm and leading him outside to leave us in peace – at last.

After three days of hard travelling across some pretty heavy terrain and an afternoon's drinking with some equally heavy Mongolians, we were in need of a rest. However, the scenery in and around Khatgal was so impressive that we decided we should take a walk to enjoy the sunset. The river was still frozen with a large sheet of ice that wound towards Lake Khovsgol encompassing several boats and even a small island in the middle of the solid stream.

To fully appreciate the mountainous scenery we climbed a wooded hillside topped with a small shrine bedecked in blue silk, from where we could watch the sun descend below the western horizon. The orange sun created a mesmerizing effect on the ice below with its reflected light looking like a giant natural kaleidoscope. As the final shards of light disappeared, we decided to head back down the slope grabbing some firewood on the way.

Having spent the two previous nights in drafty hotel rooms, it was a welcome change to be back in the cosy atmosphere of a ger and we soon had the fire roaring inside the stove, which made our felt-covered circle toasty warm. Once again, the key issue was to make sure none of the warm air inside was allowed to escape, which meant trips to relieve ourselves or to brush our teeth were very speedy affairs with the door quickly closed behind those who ventured outside. Thankfully, these efforts to retain the heat worked well and the ger was beautifully warm as we drifted off to sleep.

We had already learned that whilst nights in a ger can be wonderfully warm, if no one had woken to stoke the fire in the wee small hours, the mornings could be a little too cold for comfort. This was the case again with all three of us noticing the fire had gone out, but none of us too keen to sneak out of our sleeping bags long enough to rejuvenate it. Eventually, though, we mustered the energy to grab some wood and begin to cook breakfast. We had no major plans for the morning, the only thing on our agenda was a meeting with Ochi (Who we had met the day before) that evening to see if we could arrange for him to take us horse trekking to the lake.

When we had spoken to Ochi the previous evening, we harboured ideas of getting our expedition underway straight away. Unfortunately, he informed us there was no chance of this happening. Ochi was a strict adherent to the traditional Mongolian practice of sending his animals out into the countryside for the winter to save himself the cost of feeding and keeping them. With us being the first visitors of the year, he was still yet to venture out to locate them. This left us with a day to kill whilst he roamed the surrounding countryside in search of them.

With time on our hands and some spectacular countryside close by to explore, the equation was a pretty simple one. We would go for a bit of a hike. However, before we set off I needed to find a nice secluded spot in the woods. Gers do not come with plumbing and the local out house was a long way from being either hygienic or aromatic. This meant it was back to the old school. So, after I located a suitable tree stump and then covered my tracks with pine needles, we decided to head along the west bank of the river to see what the Khovsgol National Park had to offer.

Back in Ulaan Baatar when we had planned our expedition, we were all aware that the area would quite likely still be pretty cold. But, up until we arrived in Khatgal, I had still been confident of going for a dip in one of the world's clearest and crispest freshwater lakes. My plan had obviously been foiled as it was still pretty much frozen solid, but the vast sheet of ice did at least offer a suitable alternative for experiencing the lake at close hand.

Even though the spring thaw had just begun to set in slightly in some places close to the shore, the majority of it was still remarkably solid. We sensed that this could provide an awesome photo opportunity. So, Fran and I stepped out onto the ice and shuffled tentatively away from shore for Mitch to take a snapshot. The ice seemed to get thicker and sturdier the further out we trod, leaving us wondering whether it would have been possible for us to walk all the way across. As unusual a hike as this would have been, we thought better of it since we knew that if things went wrong the nearest medical facilities were a long way away and we had already seen the local physician at work the previous day. He did not inspire too much confidence, so we decided it would be wise to move back to the shoreline and continue our walk on the river bank.

A couple of miles further on, we came across what was a pretty common sight in modern Mongolia: a Communist relic being left to rot. When we visited the Gobi, we had seen antiques from the Soviet military presence. But, in the frozen north we saw the crumbling remnants of its economic role in Mongolia.

Alongside the pristine unspoiled frozen waters, sat a large disused water purification plant, which once probably served much of Mongolia and maybe even some of the Soviet Union with fresh drinking water. However, it was no longer in anything like working order. The pumps and pipe-work were all rusting and collapsing onto the ice, whilst the buildings were fighting a losing battle against the elements and were crumbling down towards the water's edge. The entire area had a distinctly ghostly feel about it as the wind howled through the abandoned water towers and across the deserted harbour. Everything around had the atmosphere of a grave-site, there was even a fitting epitaph engraved into the stonework of the dockside, reading CCCP-Mongol.

As interesting as the ruins were, they were overshadowed by the awesome scenery, which, after all, was what we had travelled so far for. We continued in the direction of the lake and eventually found the first break in the ice a mile or so further on. We wandered onto a tiny peninsula that jutted out into the water for around thirty meters. The land gradually gave way to a beach of white pebbles, which fell away into the deep icy waters.

It was clear to see why the lake was known as the Dark Blue Pearl as the water was perfectly clear and took on a deep blue tinge as the rocks descended further towards the bottom. I even found it possible to pick out a rock ten feet below and admire some of the smallest details on its surface. The three of us stared enchantedly into the crystal clear depths for what seemed like hours before we decided on heading back to our ger to see if Ochi had managed to recover his animals.

We arrived to the rather bemusing sight of Oyga's jeep parked a few hundred meters from our ger. Since we had only paid him to bring us one way, we presumed he had already left. But, apparently this was not the case. As we neared the ger, we saw that Oyga and the harbour-master appeared to be involved in a somewhat animated discussion. Confronted with the slightly puzzling situation Mitch and I decided to try and involve ourselves in the conversation so as to find out why our oversized ex-driver was still in town and not on his way back to his wife with his handsome earnings tucked into his back pocket.

Unfortunately, neither of them spoke English, so we were at a loss as to what was going on. To relieve this problem the harbour-master suggested we seek out Ochi to act as an interpreter. This seemed a good idea, but alas by that point he had not yet returned from the search for his animals. Therefore, we were forced to find an alternative, a young woman who taught at the local school and spoke decent English and agreed to help.

Our hastily arranged interpreter explained that Oyga had made his way into town the previous evening and had been drinking, quite heavily, according to most sources. He had taken his jeep with him on this little expedition and apparently tried to drive it back towards our ger after the local bar had closed. As he swerved and bounced away from the centre of town, the police were on hand to apprehend him. This little infraction may have caused him to spend a night in the cells rather than on the floor of our ger, but the crux of his problem was that the police had relieved him of Tg 50,000, leaving him unable to afford the petrol to get home.

In his state of newly found poverty, Oyga clearly saw us as his best option in recouping the money he had lost the previous evening. He began by making a half-hearted and particularly ineffectual attempt at claiming we should pay the fine for him, before swiftly moving on to suggesting that he could wait around a few days and then take us back to Erdenet. We did ponder that idea, but his exploits were enough to convince us against hiring him again – heaven knows what could have happened on the way back. When we refused, he began to cry and started rambling and moaning. Whilst he did so the girl looked at him intently. After a while she shook her head, rolled her eyes and turned to us. She concluded that he was either still drunk or had got drunk again and was making minimal sense. At this point, Mitch and I took our cue, shook hands with the harbour-master, thanked the girl profusely for our services and left Oyga to his whimpering.

Because his animals had proved more difficult to find than he had expected, Ochi arrived at our ger later than scheduled. When he eventually did, he had five horses in tow: his own, one each for Mitch, Fran and I and a packhorse, which would carry our bags and supplies. After my cowboy experience in Terelje I was confident of taking to the saddle once more and was keen to get my feet back in the stirrups.

Khatgal – Khovsgol Nuur

Ochirbaat arrived at around 10.30 the next morning with his freshly fed horses. Hulmaa (my horse) was looking strong and healthy. I was chomping at the bit to get back into the saddle, my cowboy hat was perched on the top of my head and a country music soundtrack was once again galloping across my brain. However, before we could set off, we had to load up the packhorse - the poor guy was set for a tough couple of days.

Each of us had a well-stocked rucksack and Ochi had brought along a tent and a stove with which he would cook. It took almost an hour of chasing, tussling and wrestling with the animal before everything was lashed firmly to his back. Once we won the struggle, we could finally set off along the river, bid temporary adieu to our ger and hopefully a permanent farewell to Oyga.

Once back in the saddle, I had no trouble picking up where I left off in Terelje and I soon had westerns playing across a movie screen inside my head. Just as in Terelje, the scenery was stunning with the big Mongolian skies once again taking our breath away. Hulmaa seemed to be a well-trained mount and he was soon off at the canter I asked of him - a winter out on the frozen steppe appeared not to have caused him too many ill effects. Mitch's steed, on the other hand, was showing some very overt signs of not having wintered so well. The animal was looking decidedly thin and was clearly not appreciating Mitch's larger and heavier frame. It really did not appear keen on breaking into anything more than a gentle stroll.

After less than a mile of our journey, Mitch was languishing at the rear and beginning to fade away into the distance. By the time we had crossed the Khatgal River and found the path towards the lake, Ochi had had enough of the lackadaisical pace the horse was taking and he galloped back past Fran and I to place an emphatic crack upon the horse's hind legs with his whip. It certainly had the desired effect, at least temporarily. Mitch suddenly drew level with Fran and I thanks to a hitherto unprecedented burst of speed. However, the animal soon began to tail off once more. Despite Ochi's best – and at times brutal – efforts, this became a recurring theme of our expedition and at no point was the poor animal genuinely up with the pace.

Ochi was a member of the old school when it came to dealing with his animals; western concepts of animal rights would have seemed alien to him. When I saw him make liberal use of the whip it certainly made me feel uneasy in a way similar to that when we were chasing wolves with Chimgee's grandfather.

However, I again felt that maybe I needed to understand the Mongolian way of life before I subjected it to my westernised values. Ochi was a horseman who lived in one of the remotest, least developed areas of one of Asia's poorest countries. Making a living was no easy feat, so he needed his animals to be well trained and obedient. In a poor area of a poor country it was, sadly, the only way to survive. Nevertheless, watching him lash Mitch's horse or seeing the strain under which the packhorse was operating was far from easy viewing especially as he was keen for us to maintain a similar approach. All through the trip our horses were always keen to dip their heads either to eat a clump of grass or take a drink. I had no problem with this since Hulmaa was working a lot harder than I was. However, Ochi instructed us that whenever the horse stooped low enough to begin any form of consumption we should haul back on the reins. Apparently, a hungry horse works a lot harder than its fuller lazier counterpart.

Whilst riding the horses was immense fun for the three of us, it cannot have been too much fun for them. However, no matter how heavy our horses thought we were, their workload was nothing compared to that of the poor packhorse. It was laden with a cargo that was not only heavy, but also immensely cumbersome. Our rucksacks overhung at both sides and, after just a few miles, he was beginning to sway like an Ulaan Baatar drunk. Whenever we hit the slightest of slopes, he would slow to near a crawl. Regardless of the heavy cargo, the poor animal failed to get any sympathy from its master. Ochi had his own horse strapped to its cargo-bearing compatriot, giving him every opportunity to reach across and put his whip to use whenever the pace slowed.

We were heading for a small clearing at the very mouth of the Khatgal River where it flows - or would flow were it not frozen - into the main body of the lake. Ochi had recommended the little nook because of its scenic potential and the sheltered camp-site it offered. The banks of the lake were a day of trekking away, so both ourselves and especially the horses needed a couple of stops along the way.

We took our first break at around noon. Ochi had brought along snacks and was also keen for us to sample water from one of the thawed chinks in the river. So, we dismounted for a brief sojourn and allowed our horses some brief respite. With six or seven hours in the saddle still ahead of us, Ochi warned that our stoppage could not be a long one for fear of losing light before we reached the lake. This was fine by us, but the packhorse did not agree and as soon as we had stopped, he slumped to the ground in a rucksack-covered heap. This was all well and good whilst we munched away on bread and sipped our icy cold river water, but it posed a problem when we were ready to leave and the animal did not want to budge.

Ochi began the process of getting it to its feet by slapping it on the hind legs and attempting to forcibly drag it up. Unfortunately, the horse showed way too much resilience to yield that easily. So, after much shouting and some further slapping the three of us were drafted in to help. It took a good ten minutes of tugging, grunting and sweating before the packhorse was up and we could get back on our respective mounts.

Despite the tribulations of our first stop-off, our second was much more substantial. We had begun to hit some heavy woodland along the way and were making painfully slow progress across the soft ground. So, Ochi directed us towards a farm owned by one of his buddies. When we arrived, it was deserted. To fill the time until his friend arrived, Ochi began to explain the techniques behind herding and keeping animals in such harsh areas and under such extreme temperatures.

In May, the herder's ger and the animal pens that accompanied it, were sat on a southern facing hillside. This afforded shelter in the winter months when bitterly cold northerly winds whipped over the lake from Siberia. He estimated that in a month or so it would be warm enough for the farm to be moved onto an opposing slope. In summer, the north-facing incline would offer the animals a cooling breeze when the sun beat down from the cloudless blue sky.

When they arrived back from tending to their animals, the herdsman and his son served us traditional Mongolian tea and dried bread. Their home was nothing like the gers we had visited in UB or the one in which we stayed during our trip to Terelje - this was the real thing. It was even far more basic than the harbour-master's ger, where we had spent the previous two evenings. From the inside, it looked almost skeletal. It was clearly built for function and nothing else with half of the interior fenced off and used as a pen for a newly born goat. The animal was the first birth of the spring and was still too weak to face the cold world outdoors.

We stayed with the herdsman for two cups of tea and just over an hour. Even though watching the baby goat taking its first tentative steps was great fun, we had to hit the saddle and make for the shores of the lake once more. For the remainder of the trek we were mainly weaving our way through thick but largely leafless forest. Ochi again blazed a trail from the front whilst we just managed to keep him and the ever-weary packhorse in view. The forest floor was soft and orange, covered with fallen leaves and pine needles. The going was slow, but relatively easy. Our greatest hazards along the way were the fallen, decaying branches strewn across the ground. Hulmaa took great pains in avoiding these by either skipping over or lurching around them. In the process she began to cause me a lot of discomfort all the way up my legs, which started to bruise more and more over the course of the afternoon. Keeping one's self, steady on a small horse travelling over bumpy ground involved a lot of legwork and left my inner thighs and calves exceptionally tender.

The majority of our trek was along the eastern bank of the river. This allowed us to look across at the vast expanse of mountains and hillside forests on the western shore where the constant winter gales had caused a curious effect on the mountainsides. The trees on the slopes that faced towards Russia in the north were dark and leafless, whilst those that looked south towards the rest of Mongolia and then onto China were still lush and green. When I questioned Ochi on the curious sight he could offer no concrete explanation, only that the weather that came down from Siberia across Khovsgol could be harsh.

It was a relief to my body when, in the early evening, we began to hear the whistling wind coming in over the shores of the lake. We still could not see the lake proper, but it seemed to spur Hulmaa on for one last push. His head began to bob heavily as he sensed a good long rest was not far off and he seemed to have found a new lease of life that soon brought us to a gentle slope that led to the banks of the lake.

All in all, it had taken us five days to reach one of Asia's greatest natural assets. By that point, we had already travelled by train, jeep and finally horse. The expedition had taken in some cold and unpleasant hotels, cold and unpleasant food and we had been denied sleep at every possible turn. However, it was worth it. As our horses gradually came to a standstill we looked out across a vast field of ice that stretched away into the distance and for miles beyond. The combination of white, grey and silver had an almost serene beauty to it. The little spot to which Ochi had steered us, brought a sense of peace and cleanliness that I had not before experienced in Mongolia.

The mouth of the river was heralded by a short rocky peninsula, which jutted out into the ice. We climbed towards the top of the outcrop and out into the frozen beginnings of the lake. At the very tip was a small shrine made up of carefully placed rocks and the obligatory blue silk that Mongolians love to place on sacred places. The fabric was being blown horizontally and almost rigid in the wind. The howling was so strong that we could barely manage to speak to each other. However, this was fitting really, I don't think words would have done the view any sort of justice. Instead we just stood and stared.

We savoured the view for as long as possible, but after a while practicalities began to set in once more. It was evening, the sun was beginning to set and we still had nowhere to sleep. Therefore, it was time to put up our traditional Mongolian tent. Everyone pitched in, but in truth our duties proved to be relatively modest with Ochi doing the lion's share of the work whilst we were relegated to fetching, carrying and lifting. It was a true spectacle to watch a genuine expert at work. All he had carried with him was the fabric of the tent; the rest he made himself from what he could find in and around our camp-site.

He fashioned the poles, pegs and supports from fallen branches and logs that he found on the forest floor. The poles came from two fallen boughs, each of which was around four feet in length. He hacked away at both ends of the first piece to produce a spike at the base and a v-shaped cavity at the top. The second bough slipped into the freshly made crevice to form a giant T, around which our home for the evening was draped. From there we stretched out the canvas to form, the shape of the tent. We then pinned it down with pegs made from a series of smaller fallen branches.

As impressive as Ochi's skills in the outdoors were, the wind was still biting and an expansive frozen lake was only twenty feet away. The canvas looked flimsy and no match for a cold Khovsgol night. I was beginning to get some more rather unpleasant flashbacks from my early morning wake-up at Manzshir Khiid. Then, Ochi unearthed the tents' special feature. It was an inbuilt cooking and heating system: the stove. It had been transported as a series of metal plates and tubes carried by the packhorse. However, in a matter of minutes it was brought to life and was pumping wood smoke through a specially placed hole in the top of the tent.

With the stove burning away happily, it was time for dinner. The meal we ate by the shores of the lake was by far the best food I ate during my entire stay in Mongolia. Ochi had brought dried mutton and rice, which proved to be the first meal I had cooked for me by a Mongolian where the meat was lean and not swimming in fat. It was simple, but delicious. Ochi was excelling himself, both in the erecting of the tent and also in his cooking. Yet his handicrafts did not stop there, they even extended to the cutlery with which we ate our meal. Instead of carrying the extra weight of forks and spoons he simply found some nice clean wood, took his knife and carved us each a set.

Once the mutton had settled in our stomachs, it was time for a solo foray into the darkened woods. After I located and utilized a suitable tree stump, it was time for bed. Regardless of the stove and the heat it was providing, I was taking no chances with the cold. I climbed into my sleeping bag fully clothed with a set of thermal underwear beneath my outer garments. Ochi, on the other hand, simply had his Del.

In UB, the Del served simply as a coat and also traditional dress. It may have been cold on the city streets, but out in the country the national dress went from being merely an elaborate and thick overcoat to a key piece of survival equipment. The design ensured Ochi could face-off the harsh Siberian weather with confidence. The thick fabric of the Del wrapped twice around the front and fastened with a belt at the side whilst the sleeves were long and overhung past his wrists to keep his hands away from the elements. When it was time to turn in for the night, all he did was take off the Del and use it as a thick, wide blanket into which he could happily roll himself.

After tucking myself firmly into my sleeping bag and getting nice and snug, things seemed to be going swimmingly. However, as we began to doze off, I noticed that the flaps at the mouth of the tent were still pegged open and the cold was beginning to drift into our nice warm little nook. To remedy this, Ochi reached out from under his Del and pulled them closed. Unfortunately, where this solved one problem, it exacerbated another.

The smoke from the stove was, in the majority, being puffed out through the chimney and the hole in the roof. However, only a few hours earlier the stove had been a series of metal plates being carried by the packhorse. These had slotted together well, but Ochi had not succeeded in making them completely airtight. Consequently, some of the smoke was managing to escape through the thin gaps between the panels. Whilst the flaps were still open this was no big deal, but once they were closed there was nowhere for the stray fumes to go. Within only a few seconds we were all spilling from the tent coughing violently and rubbing our eyes.

Despite spending the entire night with the tent flaps open, there was no repeat of Manzshir Khiid. Thankfully, the cold never became a major factor and the stove ensured we had a comfortable night's sleep. Ochi woke three times in the night to tend to his horses and each time he did so made sure the fire was still going. We were, however, woken at first light by yet more howling winds coming across the lake. Whilst the Mongolian weather in May was relatively mild compared to deepest winter in UB, the wind chill gave the effect of sub-zero temperatures.

Because of the cold and windy world outside, I was somewhat reluctant to leave the warm confines of my sleeping bag. However, the call of nature, the need to brush my teeth and the prospect of a well cooked breakfast managed to rouse me from my slumber. For our first meal of the day Ochi again used dried mutton, this time it was served with noodles and once more it was delicious.

With breakfast finished, everything we had carried with us had to be loaded back onto our horses. Hulmaa and the other horses that carried Mitch, Fran and I were in for a slightly easier ride as we had eaten all the food that had been in their saddlebags. The same was not true of the poor packhorse however. The ailing beast was soon struggling his way back up the slope that had brought us to the shores of the lake under the same weight of our rucksacks and Ochi's tents.

The trip back was far slower than the journey out. As we made our way back along the east bank of the river, our animals finally began to show some signs of the harsh winter break they had just endured. The slower pace we were taking meant that if we wanted to be back in Khatgal before nightfall, we had no time for any prolonged breaks. So, it made for a long uncomfortable day in the saddle. By the time we had crossed back over the river, both Hulmaa's energy levels and mine were dropping. He was content to amble the final mile of the trip and my legs were in no condition to deal with him going any faster.

The light was fading fast when we approached Ochi's homestead. The weather had turned frighteningly cold and I was in pain from my slightly swollen ankles all the way up to my bruised and aching thighs. It was a massive relief when we could dismount and enter Ochi's cabin to enjoy some noodle soup freshly cooked by his wife.

Khatgal - Erdenet

We woke on Saturday morning with the question of how we would get back to Moron and then beyond at the forefront of our minds. Oyga was, thankfully, nowhere to be seen. His antics over the past few days had left us cautious at the prospect of travelling all the way back to Erdenet in his company. Thankfully, a better solution presented itself quite quickly. The harbour-master had a friend who owned a jeep and could take us to Moron at around lunchtime. So, we packed our bags, stuffed them into the back and headed off across the steppe once more.

As we blazed our trail along the dusty, bumpy, rutted roads I began to wonder what had happened to Oyga. Our unpredictable, alcoholic former driver could have been anywhere. I presume he eventually made his way back to Bulgan. I also imagine that when he arrived back he got a massive dressing down from his wife. After all, he had lost the spoils of his lucrative trip. It may well have been a couple more months before he had the chance to take any more westerners as far as he had driven us.

Even though our driver had changed, the terrain remained the same. We bounced, rolled and swayed our way across the country at an agonizingly slow pace for almost three hours before the telephone wires finally led us onto the dusty streets of Moron. Once we had been dropped at the jeep station we were torn between two schools of thought over what to do next. The first was to be satisfied with how far we had come in the day.

If we decided that reaching Moron was enough for us, we had the option of finding somewhere to stay and then travelling through the day on Sunday to reach Erdenet by the evening. However, on the previous occasion we had been in Moron, entertainment and accommodation options were limited. This consideration began to push us towards our second option. We could climb into a minivan right then, drive through the evening and get to Erdenet nearly a whole day earlier. The only downside was the possibility of arriving in the dead of night.

Despite the outside chance of freezing to death on the streets of a Mongolian mining town, we decided to risk taking our chances there and then. The thought of a day in a cold hotel in Moron eating cold mutton was just too much for us! We all hoped that if we made good time we could make Erdenet before midnight and find somewhere decent to stay. We were perhaps being a little optimistic.

After we had loaded our gear into the back of the minivan, the prospect of making Erdenet at any kind of reasonable hour began to fade rapidly. We sat idly in the back seat for almost two hours while the driver waited to fill up every single spot. He was not happy until all the seats and even a small plastic stool he had added were occupied. When a full quota of passengers was crammed in like sardines, the journey finally began ... at least temporarily. After travelling a whole mile we then stopped for gas and supplies. It was early evening when at last we got out of Moron and were onto the steppe once more.

The passengers on their way to Erdenet were a mixed bunch. Obviously the foreigners crammed into the back seat were the most unusual and were subject to prolonged stares of curiosity and hushed conversations. However, despite our novelty value, we managed to avoid being the major centre of attention. That privilege belonged to a short, ugly and exceptionally drunk man in his early twenties named Bira. He had a seat on the row in front of us, but instead of using it in the conventional manner he was kneeling up and facing the back of the vehicle where we were sitting. Together with his equally ugly, but considerably less drunk friend Dolgsuren he seemed fascinated with everything about us.

We attempted to make some basic conversation, but unfortunately met with only minimal success. However, when Mitch unearthed his phrasebook things moved up a gear. Bira quickly snatched it away and began pointing at various words and phrases to make some basic questions. We responded by finding the appropriate words to answer his enquiries and pointed at them in a similar vein. This went on for almost an hour until Bira had, it seemed, exhausted his curiosity. Unfortunately, once he could think of no more new questions he decided that the best option would be to ask the old ones over and over again. I told him that I was twenty-four, from England, single and a journalist at least six times. Thanks to their drunken pointing, we discovered that Dolgsuren was a police officer in Erdenet and that Bira wasn't much of anything. We also discovered that a middle-aged lady sitting in the front row, wearing a pained expression was Bira's mother.

As part of our efforts to blend in we had bought a small bottle of vodka along with us. Once Bira caught a glimpse of this, his eyes lit up and he insisted we shared it with everyone. The 500ml didn't last long. We sipped the first few mouthfuls slowly, before Bira chugged the remainder at pace. We hoped that once the bottle had been emptied he would settle down, fall asleep and leave us in peace for the remainder of the journey. However, having had plenty of experience with Mongolia drunks we should have realized that that was never going to happen. The questioning and staring did lose their intensity as Bira slipped sporadically into unconsciousness. Unfortunately, whenever we hit any sort of bump - of which there were many - he was jolted back into life and would begin pointing at the phrasebook once more.

Whilst Bira's antics were amusing and only mildly annoying for us, the rest of the bus was holding him in pure contempt. An unfortunate gentleman dressed in an ageing but nevertheless quite smart suit bore the brunt of the drunkenness. Each time Bira lost one of his many battles against unconsciousness, he would slump into the man's lap and begin to snore. The situation reached a crescendo when our vodka-swilling friend fell comatose across the man's lap with the bottle still in his mouth. He was quickly roused so that the man could swap seats with an unimpressed mother.

Night began to fall as we ploughed our way across the steppe. As the last embers of the sun disappeared behind us, we began to worry that we would struggle to make Erdenet before some point when it would be too late to find anywhere to stay. It was around eleven when we made our first major stop of the journey. We arrived at a ramshackle guanz in the middle of nowhere and sat down for a meal of rice and mutton. The tables were dirty, the food was cold, but worst of all we learned that it was only half way to Erdenet.

After we polished off our none-too impressive meal, we all piled back into the bus for phase two of the journey. As we stepped back on-board, none of us had any idea how bad the remainder of the trip would be. I can confidently say that the subsequent eight hours were some of the most tiring, uncomfortable and unpleasant of my life. After the meal Bira had made his way to the back of the vehicle and wedged himself between Mitch and I. This left four of us squeezed into what was originally a small seat for three people.

Bira's presence in the middle of us pushed me off the edge of the seat, or at least halfway off the edge. I wound up travelling over 200 kilometres with one buttock cheek perched precariously on the cushioned seat and the other squashed against the cold metallic wheel arch. I felt so cramped that at times the only way to stretch any of my limbs was to open one of the side windows and allow my right arm to dangle along the side of the bus. Both legs and my left arm were deprived of the luxury of movement.

The best way to escape such discomfort would have been to arrive in Erdenet. However, that prospect remained a long way off. With the landscape darkened, we would be forced to drive far more slowly with no idea when we would arrive at our destination. As we moved further into the dead of night, I began to have mixed emotions as we swayed over the pitch-black steppe. On the one hand, I desperately wanted to make it to Erdenet as quickly as humanly possible so that I could end the almost unbearable discomfort and give my right buttock some desperately needed rest. Yet, I was not sure that I wanted to arrive there at four or five a.m. The city is quiet and lifeless at the height of the day, in the early hours it would have been dark, deserted and treacherously cold.

The only alternative to the extreme discomfort of the back seat would have been to escape through sleep. However, just as on every car journey I had taken in Mongolia, that proved close to impossible. Our driver could see only as far as his headlamps pierced into the darkness and had no idea where the nearest rock, trough or divot would be. Any time I began to edge towards a nocturnal escape, the minivan would bounce around on the road and I would be thrown across the back seat with alarming force. The fatigue and frustration at the whole situation was beginning to show, especially as Bira was sound asleep and happily snoozing against Mitch's shoulder. The big Canadian was, like Fran and I, not enjoying the discomfort and sleep deprivation. He looked across at me and speculated that Hell may well have been quite similar to a through-the-night minivan trip in northern Mongolia. I could understand his viewpoint.

We had set off towards Erdenet at just after three in the

afternoon. At just before eight the next morning we, finally, got there. In that entire time, I managed somewhere around forty-five minutes sleep. So, when we rolled onto our first major road for nearly six days and five hundred miles I was relieved beyond measure, but didn't really have the energy to muster too much enthusiasm.

When we arrived in Erdenet the previous week it was snow-covered, cold and closed. This time it was wind-swept, cold and deserted. The minivan dropped us in the centre of town and we were left to our own devices. Even with the greatest initiative in the world however, we would have been unable to find food shelter or accommodation – the entire town was closed. The closest we came to anything that looked remotely open was the town's main hotel. The doors were unlocked and there were staff inside. Unfortunately, this was merely a ploy to raise our hopes of a warm breakfast - the restaurant and all the other facilities were closed. Having searched Erdenet from top to bottom we decided that there was nothing else for it but to sit and wait outside in the cold until something opened.

At some point past nine o'clock, after over an hour sat shivering in the town square, a small coffee shop finally opened its doors. The wait had seemed like an eternity. We slumped into the chairs and settled down to several cups of coffee followed by a plate of mutton and rice. It was, once again, the only meal on the menu. Regardless of the lack of variety, the little coffee shop served us well. We hung around in its warmth for close to two hours whilst the temperature rose a little and a few other establishments opened.

Whilst we were keen for pretty much anything to open its doors, both Mitch and I were desperate to get into one place in particular: the local Internet café. Mitch wanted to know the outcome of the Toronto Maple Leafs play-off series against the Philadelphia Flyers and I was wracked with nerves and tension over the outcome of QPR's promotion challenge. The Superhoops had played their decisive final game Saturday afternoon English time, early Sunday morning local time, roughly seven or eight hours before our arrival in Erdenet.

There were three Internet cafes in Erdenet. Two appeared to be closed permanently, but the third opened its doors around eleven. It was safe to say we were their first customers. The news from Canada was not good; Philadelphia had sent Toronto crashing out. The result from England was a far better one though. QPR had beaten Sheffield Wednesday 3-1 at Hillsborough and in doing so secured the three points needed for promotion. I would, ordinarily, have been at the game as Hillsborough was only 15 minutes from my house. It certainly hurt not to be at such a major occasion for my team - and we don't have too many big occasions - but I felt being in the wilds of Mongolia was a decent excuse for my absence.

I'd had bouts of homesickness in UB, but nothing where I ever genuinely wished I were at home. However, when I thought about the discomfort on board the minivan I was in at one o'clock that morning, then compared it to the delirium thousands of QPR fans were feeling at the very same moment, I did feel a pang of sadness. I consoled myself with the fact that I had all summer to enjoy both the victory and some awesome memories of Mongolia. Discovering we had won promotion was the highlight of my day. It would have been the highlight of almost any day. However, once I had discovered the news and we had all checked our email, we were left with little else to do. Our train left for Ulaan Baatar at 19.15 that evening, so we had plenty of time to kill. We had already ascertained that there weren't many sights to be seen in Erdenet. So, we took the tried and tested option in alleviating the boredom – we went in search of a bar. We managed to find The Casablanca, a well-stocked joint that was clearly a home from home for many of the mining executives and foreign engineers employed by the local plant. The three of us lazed away the afternoon with some cold beer and dated music videos on the big screen TV.

As welcome as those particular luxuries were, it was the clean, plumbed toilet complete with sink and soft toilet paper that really grabbed our attention. The last decent facilities I had used were at the Batmunkhs apartment back in UB. The bathroom on the train was made of cold steel, had no paper and emptied straight down onto the tracks beneath. The accommodation we found in Bulgan did have a plumbed in facility, but the seat was not attached to the bowl making for a precarious process. Things had got worse from that point on. In Moron, the cold bathroom was bereft of a seat and the sink emptied into a rusty oil drum. Once out of Moron it was back to basics. The water we had used for washing came from Lake Khovsgol and if nature called we answered her in the woods. The sophistication in the Casablanca suddenly had me dreaming of a hot shower and my hair clippers, both unfortunately were still a train journey away in UB.

As we sank our final round of beers, the clock began to tick towards six and so we decided it was time to head for the station and get tickets for the journey home. The platform could not have been more different from the first time we stepped onto it. Whereas the previous week it had been wind-swept, snow-covered and totally inhospitable, it was now warm, bathed in the newly emerged afternoon sun and looking almost picturesque.

We settled into our soft-seat compartment a few minutes before seven, opened our playing cards and prepared to while away the first few hours of the journey. All three of us were looking forward to a good night's sleep. However, as I tucked myself into my bunk, I was a little reluctant to close my eyes. I knew that when I awoke the next morning we would be back in UB and my Mongolian adventure would be almost over.

ABOUT THE AUTHOR

Paul Bacon spent thirteen years living and working outside his native UK. This included time in Mongolia, Korea, China, Turkey, Oman, France, UAE and Germany. He was managing editor of Network HR, a business magazine published in China and contributed to the independent Chinese news site Echinacities. He now lives with his wife Tracy in Sheffield. This is his first book.

Printed in Great Britain
by Amazon

10501064R00129